BILL'S
BOOK

BILL'S BOOK

BILL LIVELY

iUniverse

BILL'S BOOK

iUniverse books may be ordered through booksellers or by contacting:

iUniverse
1663 Liberty Drive
Bloomington, IN 47403
www.iuniverse.com
1-800-Authors (1-800-288-4677)

ISBN: 978-1-4917-5462-7 (sc)
ISBN: 978-1-4917-5797-0 (hc)
ISBN: 978-1-4917-5463-4 (e)

Library of Congress Control Number: 2014921365

Print information available on the last page.

iUniverse rev. date: 05/27/2015

Dedication
To the
Memory
Of
My Soulmate
NANCY
April 28 1932 April 7 2014

January 6, 1953

CONTENTS

Prologue ix

Chapter 1: 1930 - 1941 1
Chapter 2: 1942 – 1950.. 7
Chapter 3: 1950 - 1955 26
    University Of Louisville 9/50 - 8/51 26
    9/51 -8/52 31
    9/52 -9/53 35
    9/53 - 4/55 38
Chapter 4: 3/1955--8/1959 44
    Patrick AFB, Florida 3/55-10/56 44
    Neubiberg AB, Munich, Germany - 11/56 - 2/58 50
    Lindsey Air Force Station, Wiesbaden 2/58-10/59 55
Chapter 5: 11/59 -- 3/65 61
    Scott Air Force Base 11/59 - 1/62 61
    Memphis Resident Audit Office 1/62 - 7/63 66
    Kincheloe AFB 7/63-6/64/ 68
    Michigan State University 6/64 - 1/65 71
Chapter 6: 1965 -1967 73
    Wheelus AB Tripoli, Libya.. 73
Chapter 7: October 1967 - March 1970................................. 116
    Barksdale AFB Bossier City, Louisiana 116
Chapter 8: April 1970 - September 1973 127
    Washington, D.C. 127
    USDA Food Stamp Program.. 130
    Maryland FSP 133

Chapter 9: September 1973 - May 1976 138

    New Orleans, Louisiana 138

Chapter 10: Kentucky May 1976 - March 1985 147

Epilogue 153

Prologue

I have often wondered who my ancestors were, where they came from and what they did. The Lively genealogy publication and Adam Nicolson's book "God's Secretaries" state that Edward Lively was one of the English scholars who translated the King James version of the Bible. The genealogy also shows a plat of early Williamsburg, Virginia where there were three building lots owned by a Lively. Since that time, the publication shows that I descended from a Mark Lively who lived in the 1700s. There is little information concerning what he and his descendants did until the present time. There is some information concerning ancestors of my Peavler and Sanders grandparents, but none on my grandmother Molly Dawson Lively. So in 2050 when Jordan, Adam or Will Zanetis; and Brittany, Rebecca, Danielle or Thomas Lively are asked by their grandchildren about their ancestors, they will have this work to fall back on.

I love my God, family and country. But you will find in this work that I also love friends made over the past 70 years, having been an auditor, and athletic competitor. As an auditor, I needed to determine the condition, cause and effect of an item being examined. The same concept pertains to life in general. The main condition in family life is the marriage. The cause is how this marriage came about. The effects are the children, grandchildren, and later descendants. I believe causes for good long lasting marriages are meant to be. In 1950, if Clark Wood had not asked me to come to Louisville to play football and Nancy's grandfather had not asked Nancy to come to Louisville to school and keep house for him, I doubt that we would have ever met and had the four children and seven grandchildren that are the joys of our lives. The same can be said of my parents because the railroad hired my Mom to be a ticket agent and she met my Dad when he audited her accounts.

Ruth Peavler let her great grandson read the first three chapters of this work and he said "If Bill's father had not gotten his nephew, Bush Peavler a job as ticket agent for the railroad at Sims, Illinois where he met you I wouldn't be here." This is an example of the effect of someone doing something for someone else.

In writing this auto-biography, I strive to use newspaper standards of determining the who, what, when, where, why, and how things occurred as follows:

Who - Family members, past and present; friends; employers; co-workers and staff; teammates; coaches; others and lastly myself.

What - These are the events that occurred during my life. Events during adolescence; college years; early married life; birth of our babies; the Air Force; USDA Office of Inspector General; and retirement.

Where - Kentucky, Florida, Germany, Illinois, Tennessee, Michigan, Libya, Louisiana, Virginia, Louisiana, and Kentucky.

When - The 1930s through the 2000s.

Why - The conditions occurred because of someone else; Nancy's and my actions; and God's will.

How - Results usually occurred because of actions taken on my part or those close to me. Creativity, following proven procedures, and sometimes lucky or unlucky practices, were how things occurred in work and life.

I have had up and down times, but with faith and trust everything worked out. After 70 years I am content and would not have changed anything in my life especially finding Nancy, the love of my life.

Further, Author Richard Lederer in his work, Comma Sense, wrote the following that I feel describes my efforts and feelings while writing this autobiography:--------" Like it or not, writing well--not artistically, not ornately, not floridly, but just competently--really is the difference between being largely able to define your own life and having much of your life defined for you. Writing is, in a word, power."

As I write this, Nancy and I look forward this year to our golden wedding anniversary on August, 22, 2003. I will continue with my story ...

CHAPTER 1

1930 - 1941

I was born in Louisville, KY. on January 10, 1930. My mother was the former Eva Opal Peavler and my father was Thomas Marion Lively. They resided at 2716 Virginia Ave. in the west end of Louisville. I had a half brother, Thomas, and half sister, Janis. They were my father's children from a previous marriage. His first wife and her baby died during child birth. Thomas was 16 and Janis was 8 when I came into the world. Thomas joined the Navy when he was 18, so I do not remember him being at home during my early age.

My dad was born December 13, 1881, the son of Henry Pierce and Mary Louise (Molly) Dawson Lively in Hart County, KY. He was the second of five surviving brothers and one sister, Ella May, who died in 1900 when she was 17 years old probably of a ruptured appendix. Dad and two brothers work for railroad companies. Thad and Stuart were lawyers for the L & N railroad and dad worked for the Southern as an auditor. Frank spent much of his life in the military and Eugene had various jobs in Louisville.

My mother was born June 12, 1888, in Mercer County, KY, the daughter of Leonard Grant and Harriet (Hattie) Sanders Peavler. Mom had a sister, Vera Mabel, and two brothers, Leonard Morris and Byron Beckham. They lived in Mayo, Mercer County in the late 1800 and early 1900s. Later, they moved to Danville, KY. Both of the brothers and Vera married while Eva remained single and worked in a department store. She lived with her mother while Leonard (granddad) was in Central America logging mahogany for several years.

1

During this time, Eva changed jobs and became one of the first women hired by the Southern Railroad to be a ticket agent at the Danville station. It was there that she met Dad since he had to audit each station bi-annually. He had lost his wife a few years earlier. Mom and Dad were married December 30, 1925 and resided in Louisville. Four years later, when Mom was 42, I was born weighing in at 10 plus pounds. I think for six months Mom thought that I was a tumor. It was a very difficult labor for her and we were both very lucky to have made it.

My dad was a railroad auditor but had a GM automobile dealership that he lost during the depression. In 1932, we moved to Beuchel, KY and I remember that neighborhood children intimidated me. Other memories of that time were of my grandfather, Henry Pierce Lively, who lived part of the time with us; and the Lively brothers reunion in Beuchel including grandfather Henry Pierce, uncles Eugene, Frank, Thad and Stuart, plus their wives and children. At this reunion, I declined to have my picture made so I've heard about it for many years from cousin Tucky. The other big occurrence while we lived in Beuchel was the night our barn burned down, and the loss of a brand new Oldsmobile in the fire.

When we moved away from Beuchel in 1934, Grandfather H. P. Lively moved in with Uncle Thad and roomed with my cousin Pierce. He told Pierce several happenings in his life that later Pierce related to me. Grandfather lived in Munfordville, KY and stood on a hill and watched the Civil War battle of Green River when he was a boy. Later he and his family, a wife, five boys and a girl had a farm near Bacon's Creek in Hart County, Kentucky. According to Pierce, the five sons did all the farming while Grandfather hung out at the Court House in Munfordville, dabbling in local politics. The boys raised corn and tobacco and had pigs and milk cows at the farm. It seems that all the boys got their fill of farming and as they left home, went to school and had other careers.

Grandfather was elected to the State Legislature in 1890 and in 1913 was selected by President Wilson's administration to become the New Mexico Land Commissioner. Uncle Stewart, the youngest son, went to New Mexico with his father and mother. Later, Pierce's dad went to New

Mexico and paid $1 for 150 acres of homestead land. He had to build a building on it. However; he did not live in it, but stayed with his mother and father for a year. He left and returned to Kentucky and his job with the L & N railroad. Grandfather returned to Kentucky after five years in New Mexico.

In 1934, we moved to Herrington Lake, near Harrodsburg, KY. My dad loved to fish and hunt, so he had my granddad, Leonard Peavler, and my mother's brothers, Morris and Byron Peavler, build us a seven room two-story home at the lake. During the next two years they built two cabins to rent to fishermen. My dad also bought two additional existing cabins on nearby lots.

We had no electricity, water, or central heat at our home on the lake so we rented apartments in Harrodsburg each winter. Janis attended school in Burgin, halfway between the lake and Harrodburg, so I also attended kindergarten and the first grade in Burgin. In 1937, Janis eloped with Ernest Hager and settled in a house on Earnest's family farm near the lake. Two years later Janis separated from Ernest and my parents placed her in a girl's school at Hopkinsville, KY. Later, in 1940 she left school and reconciled with Ernest. They remained together until she died in 1974.

After attending the first grade at Burgin, the next two years I split time at the Burgin and Harrodsburg elementary schools. After the third grade, I attended Harrodsurg schools full time except for my seventh grade at Burgin. Mom and I and several Army family renters stayed at the lake during the winter of 1942/43.

During the years 1935 through 1941, I spent the summers learning to fish and swim. I had great times when many of my parent's friends came to the lake to camp, swim, and enjoy picnics and watermelon suppers. Many prominent Baptist ministers such as Dr. Gaines Dobbins, who later married Nancy and me, came to our home to fish, eat, and relax.

From 1936 through 1939, the State was building Darnell Mental Hospital one mile away from our home. Dad rented two cabins to the families of two men who worked on this large project. There were three children in one of the families who I really enjoyed being with. They taught me to swim at Lane's swimming pool three miles down the lake. I remember the other tenant was a steel worker who earned $10.00 a day. I thought this was a fortune at that time since other folks I knew earned $10.00 a week.

Between 1935 and 1941, I was pretty spoiled, since I remember crying quite a bit and being intimidated by other children. I was short and fat, so other kids would continually tease me. I got the measles twice, and mumps once. Every summer I would get poison oak all over my body. Twice my eyes were swollen shut for days. They would give me shots for the poison oak, but the reaction to the shots was almost as bad as the poison oak rash.

Mom and I would often accompany Dad on trips when he audited railroad stations twice annually. His territory included the line from Cincinnati, OH through Danville to Chattanooga, TN, plus the line from St. Louis, MO through Louisville to Danville. Our home on the lake was seven miles from Danville, so it was the perfect location for his weekly travels. He was sure to be home on the weekends so that he could fish at his leisure and attend Church every Sunday.

Since Dad worked for the Southern Railroad, he could obtain passes on all railroads throughout the country. We took train trip vacations to California to see Thomas while he was in the navy, to Florida every winter, and other parts of the nation. We motored with friends to Chicago to see the World's Fair and drove to New York to see Thomas and his new bride in 1938. On this trip, we visited Washington, D.C. and motored through Canada to Niagara Falls. Mom and I took the train to Ridgecrest, NC to attend a week long Baptist retreat.

Recently, while taking my grandson Thomas Lively to school in Ervine, KY, I noticed a red caboose parked near his school. I remember that Dad in auditing the stations would have a train stopped and board the caboose to go to the next station or elsewhere down the line. I also remember that one night he was in Atlanta or somewhere along Southern's line on a Friday night and was due to come home on the weekend. He boarded a Pullman car and told the conductor to wake him up when he got to Lexington.

The conductor did as he was told, but when Dad looked out the window he was in Lexington, Virginia not Lexington, Kentucky. He had a hard time living that down.

Mom disciplined me with a switch but would not let Dad touch me. She felt he had been too hard on Thomas. Thomas had a very high I Q, but was always in trouble or did crazy things. Even though I was too young to remember I was told several escapades Thomas was involved in. For instance, flagpole sitting was a fad, so Thomas sat on the backyard fence post several days. He went to the west coast on a pass but rode freight cars back to Louisville. When he came in the house he had a goat with him. He also was infested with crab lice which ended up on Dad. After Dad saw the doctor, Mom made him go to a distant drug store for blue ointment. The druggist asked Dad how much he needed, so Dad said a dollars worth. The druggist replied, "That much will kill all the crabs in the west end of Louisville." So a quarters worth was all he needed. Thomas had several run-ins with the law but Dad always got him out of trouble.

In 1939, Dad bought me a steel casting rod and a Phluger Summet reel to cast for white and black bass. In 1940, he gave me a 20 gauge double barrel shot gun I used when we hunted for rabbits, squirrels, dove and quail.

In the mid thirties, Thomas had gotten out of the navy, moved to New York and married Deloris Bertrand. Soon after their marriage we visited them. In 1940, we visited them again in Norfolk, VA after Deloris had a baby boy. Thomas worked in a shipyard in Norfolk.

I was in the sixth grade in Harrodsburg in early December 1941. Dad killed a fox and several rabbits on a local farm. Later he became ill, and after several questionable diagnosis's, it was determined that he had contracted tularemia from the fox or rabbit skins. On December 7 (Pearl Harbor Day) his fever increased and he became very ill. I was with him when he was home and in the hospital, and beside his bed when he died on December 20. The doctors tried to save him but penicillin or other anti-biotics were not available then.

He may have been hard on Thomas but had been great to me. He was kind, a devout Christian, loved to have fun, a great sportsman, and enjoyed baseball and football games. I wish he could have been around when I played in high school and college. He was a friend to everyone and was a model father to me. It's sad to only have known him for such a short time. I'm sure he was the reason that I pursued an auditing career.

We had his funeral soon after he died, but had to wait until Christmas Day for the burial. Janis and Ernest had to drive in from California where they worked in an aircraft plant.

Dad left Mom a small insurance policy and the property on the lake. The next several years were hard on her, but her persistence and reliance on God's will let her overcome all obstacles in her path over the next thirty-three years.

CHAPTER 2

1942 – 1950

After the death of Dad, I still did not mature very fast. I remained a "sissy" and wanted my way too much. Mom had to go to work to support us because the railroad did not give pension benefits to dependents, even though Dad had worked for the railroad all his adult life. He would have retired five years after his death at the age of 65.

Granddad Leonard Peavler came to live with us and he became my second father. He never spoke an angry or unkind word to me. We fished and hunted squirrels together. I would listen to him for hours telling stories of his youth, his time logging mahogany in Central America, and the animals and snakes he had encountered in his travels. When he was a teenager, a neighbor who was kept up most of each night by a holy roller congregation got him to break up their meeting by pouring skunk secretion in the aisle during their meeting. Granddad said, "The last thing he heard when he went out the door was, 'this meeting is dismissed, there's a skunk under the house'." While riding a horse down a railroad track in Central America, he saw a telephone pole by the track. That telephone pole turned out to be an anaconda. He had many stories like these, that I will never forget.

Granddad owned and operated steam engines he used to thresh wheat and other grains. He used the engines to run circular saws, lathes, and other machines to make bric-a-brac that was popular in the late 1890s and early 1900s. He also used the engines to power his sawmills. Many people related that he could get more "board feet" out of a log than anyone else in the surrounding area. I was fortunate enough to be with him for a week when he ran a sawmill. He was in his late 70s, but I could see he knew what he was doing. He was a great role model and helped me grow up.

The June 16, 2002 Danville Advocate printed the following. "From our files: 100 years ago--1902. L. G. Peavler, who has a portable saw mill on the Proctor farm near Mount Mariah Church on Dick's river, had two horses fall over the cliff Friday night. Both were blind and had been turned into a field which was not fenced at the edge of the cliff. One of the animals lodged on a ledge 50 feet from the top. It is supposed it neighed and its companion in trying to find it, also walked over the precipice.

In falling it landed in the top of some trees but its struggles dislodged it and it fell on the rocks at the water's edge 250 or 300 feet below and was killed outright.

Steve Lucas and others got a block and attached it to the one on the ledge and drew it up. It had stood on this shelf for several hours with its feet within 3 inches of the edge where any movement on its part would have sent it to certain death.

The animal seemed to realize the danger to save its life, for during the time that the ropes were being placed about its body, it never moved a muscle. After getting on safe ground the poor beast showed its delight in frequent whinnies."

The older I became the more I appreciated Mom. Many things occurred during these years without my father. I found that she was hard working, had a good personality, a good sense of humor, and absolutely adored me. Later in life, I found several notes and tidbits that molded my mother's thoughts and self-being. For example, these items follow.

Love Brings Success.

Fall in love with your home or your work or the people you do
     business with or your city.
Fall in love with all of them.
No one can be a real success in any work unless he loves it.

Men rarely have been successful who have not had a single purpose in view.

Success hunters who scatter their shots generally miss everything they aim at.

I always think of three symbols typifying the threefold development of one's physical, mental and heart powers.

A spade to remind that we must first dig.

A ladder to remind that we must climb.

And a start to represent the big ideal we select for our selves to climb toward.

E.O.P. (Eva Opal Peavler)

Mom would take offense and rightly so if she was unduly criticized. In one case she kept the following postcard from the Harrodsburg Baptist Church, postmarked June 23, 1939. To my knowledge she never went back to the Sunday school class after she received it.

Because it was raining last Sunday
Was no reason for your not being there?
If only to just fill a chair.
The teacher was there with her lesson,
Prepared, ready to say her say,
But the pupil is quite as important
As is the teacher any day.
Next Sunday again we are asking
That your place in the rank you fill.
What does it matter if it is raining
You would get there for a $5.00 bill.
Silver and gold have we none.
But such as we have, we offer thee
Eternal life through Christ our Lord
It cost our Savior Calvary.

She also had a great sense of humor and wrote or kept funny items that she cut out of the Newspaper or magazines. I believe she wrote the following

From Bill,

Daddy called me William
Sister called me Will
Mom called me Billy
But the fellows call me Bill.
Mighty glad I ain't a girl
I'd rather be a boy
Without them sashes curls & things
That's worn by Fauntleroy.
I love to chunk green apples
& Go swimming in the lake
Hate to take the caster oil
They give for bellyache.
Most all the time the whole year round
There ain't no flies on me.
But just fore Xmas, I'm as good as good can be.

To Mom

Following are some of the items from newspapers, etc.
Preacher stopped and called a council,
He had baptized forty-eight
But the schoolma'am, Mandy Hounsel,
Rose above three hundred-weight.
How could a lean, five-foot preacher
Baptize her without a slip?
Think that he could lift the teacher,
What if he should lose his grip?
All the hillside, silent, wondered,
Here and there a smothered sob;
Mandy looked at least four hundred,
Standing by the Reverend Cobb
Then a poor half-witted creature,
Known about town as Shot,

Shouted out: "Say Mister Preacher,
Lead her in and let her squat!"

Boys were queer when Pa was young,
They always liked to work;
They never seemed to want to play,
And never tried to shirk;
They were so mannerly and nice,
And just as good as pie;
The wonder is they ever lived,
Since good boys, mostly die.

They never made a racket
in the house or on the street,
They never came inside the door
With dirt upon their feet;
They never stumbled over chairs,
Or wrestled in the house;
They were noiseless as a cat
That's hunting for a mouse.

When school came away they went,
As happy as a king;
And studied, my how they did dig,
To master everything;
Oft at noon they would forget
Their dinners and their skates,
And stay at their desks and work
With pencils and with slates.
They never had to be kept in
For anything they had done;
They knew what they were there for;
They did not go for fun.

I wish I'd lived when Pa was young,
Things were so different then;
For all the boys were studious
My Uncle Dan, he comes sometimes
To visit us awhile;
And when I tell him how it was,
You ought to see him smile;
He never says a word, you know,
But acts just like he thought
There were things boys did then
Which my Pa forgot!

September the two
States of the United

Mein dear cousin Hans:

I now take my pen and ink in hand to write you mit a lead pencil. We do lif where we used to lif we lif where we have moved. Your aunt what you luffed so weel is dead. She died of new monia on New Year's day in New Orleans at fifteen minutes in front of five. Some people think she had pop ulation of the heart De doctor gave up all hope when she died, her breath all leaked out. She leaves a family of two boys, two calves and two cows. Old Mrs. Offenblock is ery sick, she is at deaths door and de doctor thinks he can pull her thru. She has such a nice little boy, he is chust like a human beast. I took him to the hosbital to the sick people, we had lofly times. Your brother Gus took our dog Fido down to the saw mills yes terday to haf a fight. He runned up against one the cir lar saws, he only lasted one round. All de Grassenblock family have de mumps and are having a swell time. I am sending you black overcoats by express. In order to safe express charges, I cut de bottons off. You will find them in the insides pocket. Hans Kratz was sick. De doctor told him to take something so he went down the street and met Cohen and took his watch. Cohen had him arrested and got a lawyer. De lawyer got the case and Hans got the works. We have 30 chickens and a fine dog.

De chickens are laying six eggs a day. De dog is layin behind the stove. Just heard they formed an operation on Mrs. Offenback between de dining room and de conservator but she died between eight o'clock. De people is dying around here vot nefer died before. Hans I wish we were closer apart, I am awful lonesome since we sepa rated together. Your brudder Frank is getting along fine mit de small pox and he hopes he finds you de same. Hope you will write soon. I remain here.

Your cousin

MAX

P.X. If you don't get this letter, let me know and I will write you another von soon.

P.X. No.2 Haf just received the $10.00 vot I owe you but haf closed up de letter and won't get it in.

Mom's cousin Archie Mae Lacefield owned the apartment that we lived in and her husband later became Harrodsburg's Mayor. She recited to me the following limerick that I've remembered all these years.

There is a little Island off the coast of England called the Isle of Man,

The strangest thing about this island is that they do not use cars but ride on donkeys, commonly called asses.

Some have white asses, some have dark asses, some have ugly asses, some have beautiful asses, others have ordinary asses, while a few have extra-ordinary asses. The mayor's wife is said to have

13

the most beautiful ass in town. Often as she rides to market men stop her to pat her ass.

One Sunday morning the minister tied his ass outside the side window so he could get home early for dinner. During the service a fire broke out. Everyone ran to save his ass, the minister jumped out of the window expecting to land on his ass but landed in a hole in the ground. That shows you a minister doesn't even know his ass from a hole in the ground.

As often as I could, I visited Mom's sister, Vera Bush and her husband, Uncle Henry Bush. Uncle Henry was quite a character as he had a facade of being a very mean old man. I was really scared of him, especially when he would shake his cane and scold me. Later, I became very fond of him. At Christmas time he and I would make the eggnog and he would let me sample the "fixins." He was the Superintendent of the Lexington City Streetcar and Bus Lines, but was sick most of the time. He would have hiccups for hours, but would be well enough to call his local bookie to place bets on the races every day.

Aunt Vera seemed like a queen to me. She was about six feet tall, very erect, and had a captivating personality. In her younger years she had been an amateur golf champion. Cases of silver cups and trophies lined her walls. Uncle Henry always had breakfast ready for her when she arose. They always had a live in maid. The one I remember most was Carolyn George. Aunt Vera's son by her first marriage, Harold Bush, was a Lieutenant in the Navy serving as skipper on a small ship in the South Pacific. He had been married and divorced, and by 1942 had married Alice Ballentine, whose father founded Ballentine Breweries in New York. This marriage lasted for several years until Alice became tired of being a Navy man's wife. Harold was the pride and joy of Aunt Vera. She felt he could do no wrong and was the best looking and most courageous man in the Navy.

I was and still am impressed with Aunt Vera. During my stays there, I could take a bus downtown any time I wanted to see movies at one of five or six theaters or I could walk 4 blocks to Woodland Park where there was always a ball game or other activity I could participate in. It was easy to make friends at that age. It was also within walking distance to Stoll Field where the University of Kentucky played football. I was a die-hard fan of George Blanda, Babe Parilli, Wah Wah Jones and their football teams.

From 1942 until I was a senior in 1948, I sang several solos for plays, a wedding, the radio, and other events. Some of the tunes were: God Bless America, White Christmas, Old Man River, Going Home, Bicycle Built for Two and others. In May 1942, the Harrodsburg Herald Printed the following story: "Mrs. I. C. James, teacher of the third grade, staged a Tom Thumb Wedding for the P.T.A. The bride and groom were Betty Dean and Lawrence Willis; maid of honor, Jewell Covert; best man: Danny Wilder; bridesmaids: Lillian Dean, Ann Clark, Betty Booth Coleman, Frances Farrow; ushers: John Alexander, Mike Lowery, John McGee, James Ison Bradshaw; minister: Hollis Goodlet; brides parents: Raymond James and Mildred Brown. Billy Lively (a sixth grader) sang 'Oh Promise Me.' Thomas Hurst and Harry Carey sang a duet,'I Love You Truly' accompanied by Mrs. L. A Rice, Pianist."

During my high school years at Harrodsburg, I often played ball in T. C. (Mule) Coleman's yard on Lexington Street. I also played poker or black jack with Billy (Convict) Wylie, David (Coochie) Roach and Mule at Dwight Peavler's home since his parents were rarely there. Guys were starting to date girls, but I guess I was a wallflower since the Harrodsburg girls were not interested in me. However; over the years I became very close with many of the girls in my class; including my cousin, Mary Anne Peavler, and her friends Doris Merriman, Betty Dennis, Sitty Russell and Kathryn Sanders.

Harrodsburg decided to have football in 1946, since it had been dropped during the war years. I was a junior and at sixteen I had grown to 6'2" and weighed over 200 pounds. So I decided to give football a try. Forest "Aggie" Sale had returned from the Navy and was made head coach. Aggie had been an All-American basketball star at the University of Kentucky in the early 30s. He was an excellent basketball coach but knew little about football fundamentals or philosophy. Evan Harlow, the school's basketball coach during the war years became Aggie's assistant coach. Thus, we had two coaches who knew diddly-squat about football.

Even at sixteen, I was still scared of my shadow and often wondered if I would grow up and have some courage. Grosto Wells, a senior on the team and a star basketball player gave me a hard time when we scrimmaged or had blocking/tackling drills. He wasn't a very clean player and gave me several cheap shots, all the time running his mouth and trying to intimidate me. Sometimes he would bring tears to my eyes and I thought he was trying to get me to quit the team. At some crucial moment I became a man! I retaliated and tried to hit him in the face, the groin, or clip him on every play. It didn't take long for Grosto's intimidation actions to end.

I sat on the bench for the first two games. At one point after we were being beaten soundly late in the game, someone standing behind our bench shouted to Aggie," put Lively in the game." Aggie turned around and said that he was saving me for more important games. I felt like crawling under the bench. During the third game I did get in late in the second half. To everyone's surprise I tackled a runner for a ten-yard loss. Even old Grosto came up and patted me on the back, and at that minute I felt that I was part of the team. For the rest of my junior year I played quite a bit.

Aggie concocted some surprise plays for us to run. However; I'm not sure we surprised anyone else except ourselves. It's amazing that we managed to win three of our nine games that season.

In 1947, we began our season with Anchorage High. We were ahead until late in the fourth quarter, when Anchorage ran a reverse play. All our team went for the fake except me. I was out there alone when Jack Thorpe (who later was on the Louisville freshman team with me) carried the ball right at me. I hit him too high and he shrugged me off like a rag doll and walked into the end zone for the winning touchdown. The game ended a minute later and I felt lower than whale dung on the ocean floor.

I remember standing in the gym with a friend from Louisville who came to watch us play. Aggie walked in and said nice tackle Bill and some other inappropriate remarks. I started crying and told Aggie to take football and shove it. He apologized and we never had words again. His psychology worked on me and there is no wonder that he was a legend at the University of Kentucky and the small town of Harrodsburg. He was and still is one of my favorite people.

Three games I particularly remember. In Nicholasville, they chased the cows off the field before the game. It was raining and very muddy and on the first or second play, I dove at the runner, missed him, and buried my face in a recently deposited mushy cow pile. After the game, water pressure in the locker room showers was so low the we couldn't take showers. I had to ride 20 miles back to Harrodsburg in Aggie's new car covered with mud and cow manure. At least we won the game.

At Stanford, Aggie let me play nose guard on defense with Robert Jewel Black, the town bully, playing linebacker behind me. Stanford had John Baughman, a small fellow playing center, so all night long either Robert Jewel or I jumped over John to grab the quarterback when John snapped the ball. John became a doctor and moved to Harrodsburg. We both have memories of that game. Robert Jewell moved to Indianapolis and was murdered when he was in his thirties.

Burgin had a championship six-man football team. Six-man football is like football, soccer and basketball combined since you had to lateral or pass the ball on each play. We had an open week so Aggie arranged for us to play Burgin. Aggie had me playing center for the first time and most of my snaps to the punter rolled back to him, but no punts were blocked. For my first and only time, I kicked off and the ball went ten yards into the chest of a Burgin lineman and rebounded back to me on the fly. I've never seen that happen again. Since I had gone to school there and knew everyone on Burgin's team they made a point of hitting me on every play. We won 21 to 19 despite having three touchdowns called back because we failed to pass or lateral the ball during the plays. I got out of bed the next morning and fell on my face. The amount of running and licks I received the night before took their toll. Fifty years later, Fred and Buddy Van Arsdale and Joe Green, who still live in and played for Burgin claim they won that game.

Sixty years later Jack Baily publishes a monthly magazine in the local Harrodsburg Herald weekly newspaper entitled "I Recall" reporting those events occurring in 1947. A few follow:

"Superintendent W. W. Ensminger announced that the annual awards to lettermen of the basketball teams of Harrodsburg High School were given by Forest "Aggie" Sale and Evan Harlow at an assembly of the school. Those receiving football sweaters were: Irmal Teater, Donald Dean, Billy Lively, Bob Black, James Fraser, Jack Clark, Louis Daugherty, John David McClellan, Dan Tuttle, Everett Phillips, and Glen Graves. Those receiving bars for participation in football, who had already received sweaters were; Tarzan Watts, T. C. Coleman, Gene Royalty Carlysle Garrison, Basil Gaither and Grosto Wells."

Receiving bars for basketball were; Gene Royalty, Wilbert Bugg, Bob Black, Irmel Teater, T. C. Coleman, Grosto Wells, Basil Gaither, and Jack Clark. A cheer leader's sweater was presented to Bessie Rhea Tewmey for her four years' service as chear leader. The following received bars for cheer leading: Harriet Russell, Barbara Daugherty, Jean Sanders, Dan Tuttle, Kenneth Poulter and Claude Perkins."

"The Junior class gave a banquet in honor of the graduating class of Harrodsburg High School. The theme of the party was a "Plantation" motif with decorations and costumes picturing a typical plantation of Civil War days. Southern belles and beaux were: Misses Mary Anne Peavler, Harriet Russell;. Patty Mertes, Frances Barnett, and Kathryn Sanders. The Belles were escorted by: Herman Young, Eulyn Dean, Billy Lively, Carlysle Garrison, Donald Dean, and Bacon Moore Jr. As a toast to the seniors, "C'mon Down South" was presented by Mary Anne Peavler and "Southern Hospitality" by Proctor Riggins. Then a short musical program and floor show was presented. Doris Merriman and Donald Dean were two black-faces in A Cakewalk" and a black-face duet between Billy Lively and Ester Sallee. Advisors to the Junior Class were ; Mrs. Aimee Alexander and Mr. Evan Harlow. Mrs. Ona Gritton was the senior advisor. Miss Dorothy Dean played the piano for the musical numbers. Principal J. K. Powell was present for this event and handed out various awards.

Jack Baily also stated, "Well, it's sure times have changed, for there certainly would be no cakewalks or black-faced duets today and if there were, all the advisors, along with the principal, would be fired sooner if not later."

I kept active in school activities by participating in the Junior and Senior plays and talent shows. To my surprise I was elected Football King and the coronation took place at half time during a basketball game. When they were ready to take the picture of the Queen, Kathryn Sanders, I stepped on the end of the plank used as a step to the throne. It tipped up and almost knocked me flat on my white tie and tailed seat in front of a gym full of basketball fans. It was a good thing that I was suave and didn't let little things like that bother me.

Most of the Harrodsburg girls were going steady with someone except for me, Mule Coleman, Coochie Roach, Convict Wylie, Sam Edwards and Bacon Moore. I still had a hard time getting dates, but we went to a lot of dances in other towns around the area. Several started drinking rather heavily, but most of the group I ran around with did not.

I did well in school and managed to make the honor roll most terms and semesters. My favorite teacher was Lucille Sharp Brown who taught mathematics. There were about six of us in the class of 50 who took all the math classes offered. A college boards test was given to all senior students and our six math students scored from 91 to 99 percent on the math portion of the college boards. This was a good indication of Mrs. Brown's teaching proficiency. Harrodsburg also had an excellent English and foreign language faculty. Bess Williams was an excellent diction and debate instructor. Her students won State honors almost every year and she directed all the school plays. Amy Alexander taught most of my English and literature courses. For weeks on end we would diagram sentences to learn proper sentence structure. Fifty years later, you can tell if an older person you are talking to got his/her education at Harrodsburg by the way they speak.

I started working at the Big Store (a hardware store) when I was 14 for 25 cents per hour. I worked after school and from eight A.M. to nine P.M.

on Saturdays. Mr. Archie Woods owned the store and even though he was paralyzed from a serious stroke a few years earlier, he was there every day. Mr. Woods was a good person to work for, and soon I learned how to cut glass, cut and thread pipe, mix paint and do other tasks associated with the hardware business. It didn't take long to learn there were no left handed monkey wrenches, cans of polka dotted or striped paint, or cloud hangers. One farmer came in and asked for a combinette. When I asked what it was, he replied, "a thunder mug." One day a box was sitting on the front counter and J. C. Patterson asked me to try to keep two poles on it from turning. When I touched the poles an electric jolt knocked me up off the floor. The box was a fence charger.

Rolls of wallpaper were stored upstairs in a large attic. I hated to get the wallpaper because of the bats. Once I put a washtub over my head to keep them from buzzing me. I also kept a close watch for rats when I went into the bin where seed was stored. I worked at the Big Store for three years and although I only made $6.00 per week I gained a million dollars worth of memories and experience that would benefit me the rest of my life.

During the summer months on the lake I spent many hours swinging a scythe and sickle cutting weeds on the hillside. During my leisure hours I would go fishing by myself or with Granddad. Granddad did not believe in taking water on our fishing trips. Little did I know that learning to do without water for four or five hours would help me to get through football practices a few years later. Rowing a wooden flat bottom boat a couple of miles each day developed upper body strength, which also proved beneficial in the coming years. In addition, running up and down the steep cliff to the lake several times each day was also worthwhile in building up stamina and leg strength.

Graduation day finally came in June 1948. I was sad on that occasion because I did not know what the future held in store for me. As usual I shed a tear or two, probably more, when Commencement was over and I had my diploma. Many of the girls in my class got married soon after graduation and a few classmates decided to go to college.

Mom and I drove to Campbellsville, KY where we knew the president of the junior college, Dr. John M. Carter. He had been the pastor of our Baptist church in Harrodsburg. Mom decided that I would attend Campbellsville Junior College during that meeting, so in September 1948 I enrolled there.

I generally took the basic required courses and made A's and B's both semesters. My English and Literature classes turned out to be snaps, because very few students had ever diagrammed sentences and the professor spent much of the year having us do this. I wrote a paper on Shakespeare's Macbeth, which I had read and reported on in high school, and received an A on that project. Thank goodness for Amy Alexander, my high school English and Literature teacher.

Many students attended Campbellsville hoping to become ministers or missionaries. I also considered this possibility. To my surprise, there was more cheating in the Biblical History and Background classes than any other class I ever attended. Students used crib notes often and copied other's answers on the final test of the semester. One ministerial student who lived under my attic bedroom took an overdose of sleeping pills one night and his roommate could not wake him up. We called a doctor who came to the house and revived him. Later, the same fellow in a fit of rage hit a wall and broke his hand because of girlfriend trouble. These events kind of soured me on the choice of becoming a Baptist minister.

At Campbellsville, my room was in the third story attic. One of the windows was broken and the only heat I got came through the doorway from the floor below. Needless to say when the cold winter winds blew through that broken window the blankets felt good. I never had the flu or a cold that winter, so my living conditions were not too bad.

One of the most eventful events that occurred during my year at Campbellsville was when I indirectly almost caused the Baptist Church to burn. To help pay my way to school, I got a job as janitor of this church. Early every Sunday morning I had to start a fire in the furnace. This required setting a fire with kindling and shoveling coal into it when the fire got under way. Then I had to throw a switch that started the blower, forcing hot air through the vents into the sanctuary above.

One weekend a month I went home for a visit, so I trained another student to stoke and operate the furnace when I was away. My replacement forgot to start the blower and the furnace over heated. I guess a church deacon noted the problem, got the blower going and prevented a catastrophe. Needless to say, the Church leadership decided they did not need my services. Fifty years later I learned that the Church had actually burned down in the early 1950s because of a furnace malfunction.

The only sport sponsored by the school was basketball. I went to all the home games and managed to attend many around the state. I became friends with all the players, and rode back to Harrodsburg on the weekend with some who lived in Lexington. I spent more leisure time with them than the other students.

Bernie Myers, a basketball player, who also played football in high school, and I hitch hiked to Bowling Green, KY that spring and spent a few days practicing with the football team at Western Kentucky University. I also hitch hiked with Charles Kurtz, a friend from Harrodsburg, to McKenzie, TN to try out for Bethel College football team.

On the way back from Tennessee, we caught a ride in a truck loaded with seed corn. The driver took a short cut at Bardstown, KY and drove over a bridge whose load limits were much less than what we weighed. I still wonder how we made it safely across that rickety old bridge. Someone above was looking after us.

School ended and I decided not to return to Campbellsville because Mom could not afford the tuition and I didn't see that I benefited much from my year there. I got one letter from the Western Kentucky coaches about playing football, but they said I would not be eligible because I had attended Campbellsville. I heard nothing from the Bethel coaches, so I decided to get a job.

Mom had been working for several years in the dining room at Darnell, later known as Kentucky State Mental Hospital. She knew most everyone there and also knew that much outdoor construction work was underway that summer of 1949. She asked the construction foreman if they needed help and I was hired. We built pigpens, rehabbed several out buildings and constructed a large cattle barn. I never forgot several events that occurred that summer.

The State had a barracks that housed about 30 or 40 prisoners from the State Prison. The men worked with us every day. Two prisoners were detailed to be painters. I noticed that they rolled their own cigarettes using tobacco from a King Albert can. One day they told me the tobacco was not really tobacco but was marijuana they had processed from the hemp that grew wild on the hospital grounds near the lake. I didn't know what marijuana was, except that it was illegal and a well-known actor, Robert Mitchum, had been prosecuted for smoking it. When they asked me if I wanted to try some, I politely refused and said I didn't smoke.

One other day, I was told to ride over to Danville with one of the older workers to pick up some supplies. Before we left Danville to return to work, the fellow drove to a section of town across the railroad track. He went into a house and came back with a quart Mason jar filled with a clear liquid. He told me he was picking up some "shine" for one of the bosses. I said prayers all the way back to the hospital for us not to have a wreck or be stopped by the police It would have been hard to explain the moonshine in a State truck during working hours, especially since I neither smoked nor drank.

Once we were digging telephone post holes and needed to use two half sticks of dynamite to loosen the rocks. After one blast, I started to put the jackhammer down the post hole to drill two small holes for two more half sticks. Luckily I noticed an object still in the hole after removing the rocks. It turned out to be an unexploded dynamite stick with its percussion fuse still in it. The good Lord was looking after me that day because the jackhammer would probably have set it off when I started to drill.

As a 19 year old, it was interesting talking with the prisoners. Most everyone claimed they were innocent of the crimes they had been "sent up" for. Many were serving time for murder and one fellow told me he cut a man's throat because he cheated him in a card game. During those summer months I learned the fact that crime does not pay.

After the summer work was completed, I got a job at Larry Rice's Gem Drug Store. He treated his employees well. My duties included sales, stock room clerk, and cleanup details. He also encouraged me to grow a beard for the town's 175th birthday celebration as the oldest town in Kentucky. During Christmas he had me in a Santa Claus outfit at both the Danville and Harrodsburg stores.

During my drug store days, I began adding weight because the soda fountain and candy counter loaded with chocolate drops and orange slices were readily available for sampling. I don't know why Eudora Sutherland didn't gain any weight because she had more candy and milk shakes than I did.

By August 1950, I was 6'3" and weighed 240 plus pounds. In the summer of 1950 the Korean war started. Many of my friends were getting draft notices and I considered joining the Navy.

About the middle of August, a tall, rugged, good-looking man came into the store and asked for me. He introduced himself as Clark Wood, assistant football coach at the University of Louisville. He said that two players, Jack Coleman and Amos Black, told him I might be interested in playing football for U of L. I was flabbergasted! He said that I would not be eligible immediately since I had attended Campbellsville. He suggested that I try to stay out of the Army until the second semester, January 1951. Then I could come to school to get enough credits so that I could play the following year. I told him I would try to do what he suggested, but the draft board may make my decision for me.

On September 1, 1950, I got a telephone call at the store. It was Coach Wood. He said practice started that day and the coaching staff and athletic department decided to field a freshman team. He further stated I would be eligible to play as a freshman but not on the varsity in 1950. Did I want to come to Louisville? I told him I was on my way! Eudora's husband Harold, a pharmacy student working at the Gem, later told me I was out the door two minutes after I got the call. I hope I told Larry Rice I quit.

I packed my few belongings, kissed Mom goodbye, and took the bus to Louisville that afternoon--all 240 pounds of me.

CHAPTER 3

1950 - 1955

University Of Louisville 9/50 - 8/51

My first day at U of L was like a whirlwind. I had a physical at the nurses offices in one of the three old navy barracks. My blood pressure was a little high but everything else checked out OK. Since I would be playing on the freshman team, my two coaches would be Frank Gitscher and Joe Trabue. Both had recently graduated and were assistants to head coach Frank Camp and his two main assistants: Clark Wood and J. D. Dunn.

The next morning I began two-a-day drills with the rest of the freshmen and the varsity. On September 2, I weighed 240 pounds and two weeks later I was down to 220. Even though the practices were rough, I had made up my mind that I would never leave.

After a couple of practices, the coaches decided that I would be an offensive tackle. This meant that I would need to learn the basics of blocking and know all the plays for that position. At that time, I needed to learn basic fundamentals, for instance, I had to learn how to explode from my position on running plays and drop back a couple of steps to protect the quarterback on passing plays. If a running play went on the far side of the line, I had to go down field and block a defensive back or line backer. Needless to say, I learned these techniques through repetitions of plays time after time and I was in the best physical condition I had ever been in.

After three weeks we had our first game with Fort Knox and I had a pretty good game. That season we had six games: Two with Fort Knox, two with Camp Atterbury, one with Xavier University, and one with University of Cincinnati. We won four games, tied Xavier and lost a close one to Cincinnati. I played offensive tackle for five games and defensive tackle in the Xavier game.

The games were a lot of fun, but the practices were really tough. Coach Camp did not believe in having water on the practice field and the only way one could get a sip of water was to suck on a wet towel that the whole team used.

Maury Wolford the best player I ever faced played on the varsity right in front of me most every day. One afternoon he popped me in the mouth and I lost my front tooth. He knocked out the tooth, root and all. The only other injury I had that year was in the Cincinnati game. We wore foam rubber pads and someone hit me in the side just over the pads and I got a bruised hip that kept me out of some of the game.

The Varsity won three games, lost six and tied one. Not too good of a season but the 13 to 13 tie was with Miami University in Florida. Miami was rated 12th in the Nation and was undefeated before the tie with Louisville. The team and school had a great celebration when 2000 fans met the team after the Miami tie. This was the biggest accomplishment that Louisville football had ever had. Only bad luck prevented a win, as the winning extra point near the end of the game was denied because we only had ten men on the field

While I was there, all the coaches remained. Frank Camp, the head coach, was from the old school of coaches. There was only one way to play football, his way. If a runner missed hitting the designed area that he was supposed to, Coach Camp sometimes known as the "little man" would make corrections immediately. Mistakes ended up as immediate laps around the field, laps after practice, or multiple push-ups. Not many "atta boy" comments were made by Coach. Players late for bed checks, caught smoking, or involved with other misconduct felt the wrath of Coach. Even though he was a tough, he had compassion for all his players but didn't make it evident. I had the greatest respect for Coach Camp..

J. D. Dunn, an assistant coach, was in charge of the linebackers and defensive backs. Everyone call him "hog jaws" to his back. J. D. was a nice fellow but had favorites, much to the chagrin of the rest of the team. I didn't have much to do with J. D., but had a couple of experiences with him. During my senior year we played Florida State, and I went down the field when we punted. The player who caught the punt handed it off to a player going the other way. About a second after he handed the ball off I made a great tackle on the first player. When J. D. saw the film, he got on me for not taking two quick steps and knocking both players down.

One afternoon at practice, I was going downfield to block the defensive back, Joe Nicolletti. J.D. was standing right behind Joe, and as I gathered speed, Joe jumped out of the way and I hit J. D. squarely and sent his feet over his head. He was wearing a porky pie hat that floated down to the ground. Coach Camp didn't allow cursing, but when J. D. got up, he told me to get my head out of my ass and look where I was going. As I went back to the huddle, Coach Camp and Coach Wood were still laughing.

About fifteen years later I dropped in to visit the coaches and J. D. told individuals there that he really appreciated the effort I made while at U of L and said that I played on one good leg for two years. I really appreciated those comments.

My immediate coach was Clark Wood. He coached both the offensive and defensive lines. Coach Wood would never praise anyone while he was present. One day during my senior year, I had to be late for practice because of a class. Later, I was told that he missed me not being there and implied that I was his boy.

When I was hurt he never gave up on me, and when he thought my injured knee was good enough to play, he gave me the opportunity. During my junior year, we had an off week so Coach Wood scheduled a game for those who weren't playing with the inmates at La Grange State Prison. He took us "rinky dinks" to La Grange for a game.

At half-time, about 5 or 6 inmates came down to the field and told me that they were from Harrodsburg. No one else knew anyone there so all the players called this game Lively's Homecoming.

We were ahead about two or three touchdowns at half-time, so Coach Wood decided to run only one play the second half, right through the hole that I was supposed to be blocking. After running a few plays right at him, the fellow lined up in front of me said that he knew where every play was going the rest of the game..

The next week, at half-time at Chattanooga University, Coach Wood sent me in and I started the rest of my junior and senior seasons. I continue to keep in contact with Coach Wood and play golf with him at least once each year. He was a great role model for me.

Coaches Joe Trabue and Frank Gitscher, coached us during our first year. They remain good friends. Frank left coaching during my senior year and worked as an FBI agent for years. Joe remained at U of L until he retired.

When we started practice my first year, 1950, we had thirty-two players on the freshman team. From this group, only Jim Fults, Bob Lichvar, Jim Olmstead and I graduated four years later Only a couple of those that left came back to get their degree. There is no telling how many other players came and went during my time at Louisville. Some stayed a day, some a week, others a school semester, and a few a year. Three players came to Louisville from Duquesne University in 1952. Jack Valvo stayed two years and got his degree and Joe Nicoletti and Gene Massaro got their degrees with me.

We lived in Otter Hall, one of the old Navy World War II barracks. Three of us shared a 12 by 12 foot room. My roommates were Jack Gillam, a junior guard and Bill "Smiley" Campbell, a sophomore quarterback. Jack was a workout nut and looked like Mr. America He would put 25 pounds of weights around his waist and chin himself 25 times. He had muscles on top of muscles, but he often pulled them and spent lots of the time in the training room getting rub downs and using the small whirlpool. Smiley on the other hand, was the "Romeo" on the ball team. Girls would approach him on the street and he had to fight them off.

They picked on me all the time because I was the underclassman. My bed would be short sheeted, I would have a pail full of water fall on my head when I came into my room, a balloon full of water was put under my sheet and popped when I got in bed, and several other pranks. But, I could not have had better roommates. I still think the world of them.. One time they put my bed, a cot, in the hall and locked me out of the room. I got mad and broke the door down. This got me in trouble with Coach Camp, and kept me from getting my $15 laundry money at the end of the month.

Around the first of October, Jack introduced me to a little black haired girl he had dated whose name was Nancy Dorsey. Later she became the most important person in my life, but at that time neither she nor I thought much about the meeting. I guess she didn't care much for a country boy.

I became friends with all of the football team members, but really got close to Jim Fults, Walter Crawford, Roy Pugh, and Bob Lichvar. Most of the team lived in White Hall but I lived in Otter Hall where the basketball team resided. I became friends with many of the round ballers and had lots of good times hanging out with Bobby "Goose" Brown, Chuck Noble, "Bookie" Lentz, Corky Cox and several others. The basketball team always had a good record and several of the players went on to good pro careers.

Since I had gone to Campbellsville for a year, I did not have to take a lot of the courses that freshmen had to take, such as English, History, etc. I decided to major in accounting, and started taking the first year accounting and economic courses that were required. I took an economics course taught by Dr. Jack Craf, who wrote the book that we used in this course. Jack Craf became a great friend, and helped me out and gave me good advice all through college and later in life.

My social life during my first year at U of L really improved since a few of the coeds liked athletes, so I dated quite a lot. The local bar that catered to the football team was located about ten blocks away and several weekend nights were spent drinking beer and dancing with the stag girls that flocked there. We could stay out until midnight on Friday and Saturday nights, but had bed checks at 10:30 P.M. on week nights. I blame Gillam for leading me astray.

After the first semester was over, we started spring practice in January and continued until May. I thought that practice during the season was bad, but spring practice was worse. We had a spring game with Miami of Ohio. I did not get in the game, so was worried about my status for the next season.

Coach Camp got me a summer construction job with a crew that was building the new Central High School so I stayed in Louisville with my sister Janis. The job really kept me in shape for the coming season. I worked in concrete, carried large oak boards to shore up a sand bank, and did anything that was called for. I had to join the union and made pretty good wages during the summer. I rode to work and became good friends with the superintendent who ran the job. I continued to work for him the next two summers at the school and constructing a bridge for the new Watterson Parkway.

9/51 -8/52

Twice per day drills started on September 1 and continued for three weeks and were very rough since Coach Camp wanted every one to be fundamentally sound and in good condition for the first game with Wayne State in Detroit on September 29. Only 13 of the 32 freshman from the previous year were at U of L at the start of the season. I was slated to start at left offensive tackle and Rex Warner a great hard-working senior started at the right tackle position.

We won our game with Wayne 28 to 12, and I got plenty of playing time. Late in the game Coach Camp sent in a new freshman quarterback named John Unitas. Little did any of us know how great he would become.

We lost our next game to Boston University who had an outstanding quarterback, Harry Agganis, who ran our defense ragged trying to catch him. The final score was 39-7. Harry became a professional baseball player and played in the Boston Red Sox organization. He played one summer with the Louisville Colonels. Soon after he went up to the Red Sox he became ill and died. It was a shame for someone so young and talented to have this tragedy.

The third game was in Cincinnati, with the University of Cincinnati who was coached by Sid Gilman. He had developed the belly series plays that we had not seen before. Kenny Day, playing linebacker, kept tackling the runner who he thought had the ball, but the quarterback pulled the ball out of the runners hands after he had given it to him and either run it himself or pitched it to a following back. We lost that game 38-0.

Our fourth game was in Louisville at Manuel Stadium with Xavier of Cincinnati on October 19. It was a cold night and Xavier got the ball first. They took over five minutes to grind out a drive that ended in a touchdown. I went in on the kickoff. Then on the first play our quarterback called a screen pass to the left side. I was to hold for a couple of seconds then pull out to the left and block the outside linebacker. When I hit him my left leg was extended and one of our own players fell on my knee. As a result, I tore up the lateral ligament and had a bone chip in the knee cap.

After the game I spent the night in the dorm and was taken to St. Joseph's Infirmary the next morning. A couple of days later after draining fluid from my knee, I was scheduled for surgery. However, the night before the surgery I developed a 103 degree temperature and the doctors decided not to operate but to inject me two or three times a day with penicillin. I spent three weeks in the hospital, but got to know quite a few student nurses there that took very good care of me. I had never been pampered so much before.

On an evening my mother was visiting me, Roy Pugh and his girlfriend Kaye Roberts brought Nancy Dorsey to see me. Nancy came in carrying a small flower that she had picked off a bush outside the hospital door. As they were getting ready to leave Nancy came over to kiss me on the forehead but I pulled her face down and gave her a good kiss. Mom wondered who that little black haired girl was.

Even though I was bedridden, my thoughts went out to my teammates. Coach Camp decided to start John Unitas and the difference in the offense was quite apparent. We lost the first game to St. Bonaventure in the last few seconds by a field goal, 22-21. John threw three touchdown passes.

The next week we beat North Carolina State, 26-2, then ended our season with three victories over Houston, 35-28; Washington and Lee,14-7; and Mississippi Southern, 14-13. John, the kid from Pittsburg, was outstanding as a passer and field general in these five games. Coach Camp scrapped his offense and used four wideouts and one running back much like the pro offense that is used today. Jim Williams from Somerset, Ky was the sole running back and never lost a yard in any of his carries.

During this time the doctors decided to put a cast on my leg, from toe to hip for the next six weeks. They gave me a pair of crutches and told me to get out of bed and go back to school. The second I got up from my bed I almost fell on my face. Later I managed to navigate on my crutches. When I got back to White Hall, I weighed and found that I was 180 pounds, plaster cast and all; a forty plus pound loss. I've never been close to that weight since.

I went back to classes and later went home for Christmas. Before I went home, I returned to the hospital to get my cast removed. While there I saw a small child being fitted for an artificial leg. She must have been only three or four years old. After seeing her, I gave a silent thanks to God and felt that I had no troubles at all.

I went home to Harrodsburg, and after a walk downtown on my crutches, my leg became very swollen. Mom decided that I should not be up on it so she took me to Aunt Vera's where I spent the next couple of weeks sampling Uncle Henry's egg nog and playing canasta with Aunt Vera and her friends. One day, while playing with someone Aunt Vera must not have been too crazy about, I felt a touch on my leg. Aunt Vera passed me a couple of cards under the table so that I could win. No wonder I cared for Aunt Vera so much. By the time I left Lexington to go back to Louisville I had pitched the crutches away and was walking pretty good.

When I got back to Louisville, I had to spend a week in the hospital to have therapy on the knee. I was told to do certain exercises for the next six or seven months to strengthen it.

During the spring semester, I dated a lot of student nurses and others. A buddy of mine, Warren Oates, double dated with me most of the time and we went to Cox's Lake and Tuckers's Lake swimming with the girls. A lot of the evenings were spent at Curtis's Dog House drinking beer and chasing stag girls. Warren had a Jeepster convertible that we used on these escapades. Warren was in the little theater group on the campus and later went to New York and Hollywood. He had a great career, playing questionable characters. He starred in the movie, Dillinger, playing John Dillinger, and was in many moves and TV roles over the years. The Video Movie guide of 1992, stated that, "this rip-roaring gangster film featured Warren Oates in his best starring role. As a jaunty John Dillinger, he has all the charisma of a Cagney or a Bogart." This guide listed 34 moves that Warren appeared in. I always felt that Warren just played himself in most of his movies-- a funny no good scoundrel.

One spring night the school had a street dance in front of the Administration Building. Several of the guys were making a panty raid on the only women's dorm on campus. Warren and I were at the dance but didn't get involved in the raid. Nancy Dorsey was at the dance and I asked her if I could take her home, and she agreed. That was the first time we were together and I guess I didn't make much of an impression on her because we didn't get together until the next school year.

Spring practice ran for three or four months and Coach Camp had me doing student managers work caring for the uniforms and washing socks and jocks. He told me that if my knee wasn't better I could remain on scholarship as a manager. After doing this work for four months I told Coach that I'd rather take a chance on my knee and play ball than be a manager.

I made fair grades, and enjoyed college life. I continued to run with the basketball players. Five of us sneaked in to see the Horace Heidt show at the Armory but Bob "Pete" Peterson who was over 7 feet tall was spotted by the manager and we were thrown out. Pete flunked out of school that semester because he got Fs in five courses and a D in English. When Coach Peck Hickman asked what happened Pete told him he spent too much time working on his English assignments. Pete ended up playing for the white team that traveled with the Harlem Globe Trotters.

That summer, I returned to my construction job. They were finishing up Central High School. Since I had been there the previous summer, They gave me a very easy job, carrying the pole for the engineer using a transit. I stayed at Janis's and continued to exercise my knee and run around the neighborhood to stay in shape.

9/52 -9/53

I had no idea how my life would change over the next twelve months. I'm sure it was God's will to have me to fall in love with the only girl I ever cared about and have her love me as I loved her. This love has lasted over 50 years and resulted in as great a family and rewards as anyone would ever imagine. So when two-a-day practices started on September 1, I had no thought of what was in store for me.

My knee was in pretty good shape, so for practice and games the trainer wrapped it in an Ace bandage and put a brace on it for support. I played about two minutes In the first four games with Wayne State, Florida State, Dayton, and Xavier because the coaches felt that my knee was not ready. As noted above, after our game with La Grange, Coach Wood felt that I could contribute. At halftime at Chattanooga, he put me in and I started most of the games for the next two years. We finished up with Memphis State, Eastern Kentucky State, and Mississippi Southern with a 3 and 5 record. The most notable win was over Florida State 41-14. The next time we beat FSU after 13 tries was in 2002, fifty years later.

Offensive linemen do not get much credit for what they do during a game, so I was very surprised to read the following in the Courier Journal after the Eastern Kentucky game, "Buck Lively faked the entire press box off their seats when they had already written the tackle of George Wilson down and 'Buck' knocked the would-be tackler half way across Parkway Field."

When school started on September 20, I was required to take Fine Arts courses. I had Architecture the first half of the semester and Music Appreciation the second half. When I entered the Architecture classroom I noted Nancy Dorsey sitting on the first row so I took a seat right beside her. It did not take long for both of us to know that there was something going on. I had never felt that way before. John Unitas and Walt Crawford sat in the rear of the room, and before and after class they would call out "Oh Bucky." Nancy and I sat beside each other in the Music Appreciation class. One day the professor asked who knew what pizzicato was and Nancy said to me it was plucking a stringed instrument with one's fingers. I held up my hand and answered the question. The professor congratulated me for my response. I got a B in the course and Nancy got either a C or D. She never has let me live this down.

The first time we were together was with Roy Pugh. He had a Model A Ford coupe that he, Kaye Roberts, Nancy, and I squeezed in to go on a date. Kaye and Roy went in Kay's home for a few minutes and left Nancy and me alone. Needless to say, "sparks flew" between us and we both knew that we were meant for each other.

Nancy lived with her grandfather F. C. Dorsey, so I made many bus rides to her house over the next few months. We watched TV, went to movies, doubled dated with my roomy, Dave Rivenbark, and Barbara Duerr at the local hot spots--KTs or Air Devil's Inn, and attended school activities. If you call it that, we studied together in the library or in one of Louisville's parks in Grandpa's car.

I continued to make fair grades in school, and survived my final four months of Spring practice. After Spring finals and the last day of school, I moved back to Janis's and returned to work with the same construction company. At that time they were working on a bridge over Southern Parkway for the new Watterson Expressway. It was tough working in concrete, using a jack hammer, and doing any other thing that a laborer would do. I worked there until the middle of July when I had to go to Air Force ROTC summer camp in Greenville, SC for four weeks.

The summer camp was basic training for future Air Force Officers. We did a lot of exercising, marching, barracks cleaning, bed making, shoes polishing, and griping. We fired weapons and flew in T-6 trainers. Overall, it was a good experience but I missed Nancy so much that in our few telephone calls and many letters we decided to get married as soon as I returned--before football practice in September. At the camp my best buddies were UofL teammates Jim Fults and Dick Kovanda. Jim had gotten married that summer also, and Dick was a good sounding board for me.

From camp, I flew in to Nashville, where Nancy, her mother Jessie, and sister Linda met me at the airport. Nancy and I did a lot of smooching in the back seat of the car on the way to the Dorsey's. We had about a week to plan the wedding, return to Louisville, and get married. Nancy's father, Hiram was not too happy about the whole thing but he and I had a good talk and all ended well. When I told Mom about our plans she was not very happy either and said she might not be able to make the wedding. The moment I told her that Dr. Dobbins would marry us, she changed her mind in a hurry.

Back in Louisville I had to see Coach Camp and tell him my plans. He, also, was not too happy but appreciated it that I told him of the wedding. He knew that Jim Fults and Bob Lichvar had also gotten married that summer but failed to tell him. We got the rings, called friends and relatives, obtained the license, and visited the doctor to get counseling and blood tests. I did all right when I had my blood drawn but almost passed out when Nancy was tested.

In the afternoon on August 22, 1953, Dr. Dobbins married Nancy and me in the Baptist Seminary Gardiner Chapel. Tom Ramey was my best man and Libby Harris was the maid of honor. Several classmates, relatives and friends attended the wedding and small reception at Grandpa's home. We have several pictures of the event that we have kept all these years.

Grandpa Dorsey wanted us to stay with him until I was out of school. Nancy had decided not to return for her Senior year, but stay at home and take care of Grandpa's house. Overall, staying with Grandpa was the best thing we could do since we didn't have a lot of money, he needed someone there, and we all enjoyed each other's company.

We spent our wedding night in a motel just outside of Louisville. It was great to be married and wonderful being together. The next day we went to Mom's house on the lake. Two days later, my brother Thomas called and said that he was coming through Louisville, and he would love for us to accompany him to Minneapolis. He would take us camping on the Canadian border and send us back on the streamliner, the Zephyr, in time for football practice. We readily accepted, and had a great time with Thomas and Grace. On August 31, we returned through Chicago to Louisville. At 9:00 A.M.. the next morning football practice started.

9/53 - 4/55

Marriage responsibilities were first among my priorities but I had to get through my final year of football and college. Many changes happened to the football team. We had a new University president and administration that decided to de-emphasize football, so the first thing that happened was if any player on scholarship had less than a C average his scholarship was dropped. Nineteen players were eliminated from the team; some were only one or two quality points below a C average. Only 24 veterans returned from the previous team, so we were very inexperienced The backfield was decimated from graduation and the loss of key players. As a result we had ends playing in the backfield and relied heavily on the incoming freshmen with backfield experience.

The NCAA decided to scrap two platoon football that year and have players play both offense and defense. Thus, in my senior year I played tackle on offense and defense. This was quite a change but I really enjoyed playing both ways.

At the beginning of the school year, the University transferred business students from the Arts and Sciences School to a new school of Business. Dr. John Craf was made Dean of the school. He established a student council and held an election of the business students to seat the council. The person receiving the most votes became the president. Dave Jones who later founded and became CEO of Humana, persuaded me to run for the council. I got the majority of the votes, thus I became its first president. With this job, I had to draft the by-laws and the constitution. Just what I needed during football season; being married, having tough classes and working part time.

Dr. Craf really became a great friend and knowing that I needed a job to help the finances, he arraigned for me to start working at Sutcliff's Sporting Goods Store on Fourth Street downtown. After the football season was over I worked there until I graduated in June 1954. Then, Dr. Craf got me a job at John F. Petot's CPA firm. I worked there until I entered the Air Force in March 1955.

Married life agreed with me. Nancy and I really enjoyed living with Grandpa Dorsey. We did a lot of things with our friends the Fults, Lichvars, Rameys, and Nancy's sorority sisters and their friends. A couple of times we took them up to the lake for weekends to swim and fish. Jim Fults and I caught several large carp there.

Jan our first child was born on April 23, 1954, so life became more involved. She was the prettiest baby girl I had ever seen. I'm glad that Grandpa's house had plenty of space so the addition was very welcome and everyone reveled in the new baby girl. Family life could not be better.

In September 1953, the football season started and Marvin Gay's Courier Journal column stated, "Cupid has struck the U. of L. line. Bill Lively is now married." We won the first game at Murray State then lost the next eight. I hurt my hip in the Tennessee game and sat out the last half. The next week I did not practice and did not play in the first quarter of the game with Chattanooga. Since I had not practiced, I was well rested when they put me in at the start of the second quarter. I played the best game of my career by getting over 10 tackles in that quarter and 14 overall.

After playing with John Unitas for three years I really respected him and closely followed his career. During a Harrodsburg Herald interview about John after he died in 2002, here are a few of my comments printed by Kelli Elam, Sports Columnist.

"Lively was in the huddle when Unitas took his first snap. You could just tell that he was something special, Lively said. It was evident from the first time he walked on the field. What you saw was what you got, he was a good person. He was the same on and off the field. Most people remember Unitas as a great quarterback, Lively remembers him as more - a great friend. Lively has numerous memories of Unitas. He recalls Unitas inviting him and several family members and friends to his motel room before the Colts played New Orleans. Now, ask me who I think is the greatest quarterback ever to play the game and I will definitely include the name of Johnny Unitas on my list. As for Lively, his list only has one name - Johnny U."

Now that football was over, I couldn't imagine how the rest of my life would turn out. We lost a lot of games during my stay at U of L, but I will always have memories of those times and the people I played with. Football taught me a lot of lessons: that you needed others to succeed, to keep striving to obtain your goals no matter the pressures, and personal success can be obtained even if the success of the team does not meet its goals.

Classes in my final year were all right but I did not make the grades that I should have because of work, married life, and many other outside interests. My main goal was to get through the classes and graduate. To be blunt, I was tired of school. In ROTC, I obtained the rank of major and would be commissioned a 2nd lieutenant in the Air Force on the day of my graduation. Two years of military duty at a later date was mandatory. I didn't know if I should look forward to that or not.

My days at Sutcliffe's were very good since I had a lot of experience in retail store business early on. I enjoyed selling sporting goods and respected my employers. When I left Sutcliffe's to work at Petot's my boss told me that he hated to see me go and I could have a good career with them. One day Dr. Edleman who was president of Georgetown College came in the store and asked me if I would be interested in coaching his football team. He knew me from visiting my family years before at the lake and that I played ball at U of L. I told him that I would love to but had to enter the Air Force after graduation.

Just before graduation the school newspaper, the Cardinal printed the following article.

"Two Graduating U of L Football Heroes Bill 'Buck' Lively; Well Known Tackle and Guard Mojo Hollowell"

"One of this week's Cardinal Salutes goes to Bill Lively.

Bill a senior in the School of Business, will receive his B. S. degree in Accounting this year. He is president of the recently established Business School Student Council.

Better known as Buck to most U of L students, he will long be remembered by football fans for his outstanding block of the Eastern Ky. end in the 1952 Homecoming Game. In 1950, he played as a first string tackle on the freshman team. As a sophomore, Bill was showing great promise and was well on his way to varsity stardom when he injured his knee. This kept him on the sidelines for most of the latter half of the 1952 season. In 1953 he made the tough transition from an injured player to active competition. Bill played first string offensive tackle. During the past season, he played both defense and offense, and was one of the teams top tackles.

Bill has been in the Air Force Reserve Officers Training Corps for four years and holds the rank of Cadet Major. He is a Squadron Commander.

A native of Harrodsburg, Kentucky, Bill is married to the former Nancy Dorsey, a Chi O at U. of L. They are at home at 147 N. Galt.

For his outstanding contributions and service to the University of Louisville, The Cardinal Salutes Bill Lively."

Nancy and my life with Grandpa Fay Dorsey was a joy. He had worked as a Vice President of the Liberty National Bank for over 60 years and even though he was in his late 70's he was young at heart and enjoyed life. He wrote poems and had favorite sayings like "The Skeeter and the Flea." When he found out that we were expecting, he offered us a $100 if we would name the new one Fay. We didn't but got the $100 anyway.

`His favorite food was chicken and dumplings, and could not get enough of them. When he had finished, he would hit the couch and laid there on his back with both hands crossed over his stomach. We often thought that he looked like he was dead. Later while we were in the Air Force he made it a point to visit us at all our bases, even in Germany. Nancy was like a daughter to him and we made sure that she returned from Libya to be with him just before he died in 1967.

The night before Jan was born Nancy and I went to a movie downtown. I was interested in it, so I insisted that we should remain an extra hour to see the ending again. The next day, Jan arrived in the middle of the night at Baptist Hospital. Mother and baby were in the hospital for 5 or 6 days before they came home. The grandparents came to help out for several days after Jan arrived.

I learned fast how to take care of a little one but Nancy wasn't too happy when I picked Jan up by the draw strings to her night gown. A couple of the characters on the football team shoplifted a dress and gave it to me as a new baby gift, but we couldn't use it since it was for a three year old.

On June 6, 1954, I graduated and received my diploma which still hangs on my office wall. What a great day!

I started working at Petot's making $50 per week. Not bad for that time, and in my first month learned more about accounting than I did in four years at U of L. The experience of doing things over and over again provided me a lot of insight, just like running football plays repeatedly. One of our accounts was a hospital in the coal mine area of Kentucky. Every three months the owners sent the books in to be audited and updated. I tried to balance the cash drawing account for the first time and I worked on it for two or three days before I got the balance difference to be less than $5.00. I took it in to one of the firms partners and he told me that this was the closest they had gotten to reconciling the account in years. Later I could do this task in less than an hour. Our accounts included hospitals all over Kentucky, savings and loan associations, retail businesses, automobile dealerships and various other enterprises.

John Petot Sr. was the Treasurer of Fehr's Brewery, so twice when the payroll clerk had to be away for two week periods I was sent over to do the Brewery's payrolls. This involved paying truck drivers hourly rates, overtime rates, distance rates, and other monetary incentives. That was quite a learning experience and I only had one complaint from a driver that his pay was incorrect, which was remedied. I don't know if I overpaid anyone. Fehr's was charged $10.00 per hour for my time, but my pay remained at $50 per 40 hour week. One good thing about working at Fehr's was that I could visit the tap room and have a couple of cold ones after work.

I took trips to Lexington and Paducah to audit hospital books. We only had one fraud that occurred in a business that we audited. It involved lapping funds; withholding receipts and not posting them to a persons account. By the time March 1955 came around, I had learned a lot about accounting.

On March 15, 1955, I departed Lexington on the train bound for Cocoa, Florida where I would be assigned to Patrick Air Force Base, the home of the new Space Program at nearby Cape Canaveral.

CHAPTER 4

3/1955--8/1959

Patrick AFB, Florida 3/55-10/56

I left Nancy and Jan standing at the Lexington train station as I rode the Southern Railroad Royal Palm to Cocoa, Florida. I spent the night in the sleeper and arrived the next day, called the base and they sent a car to pick me up. I received some instructions and was told that I would be working in the accounting office with some other new lieutenants. I was assigned to a room in the Bachelor Officers Quarters (BOQ) and shared a bath with a lieutenant from New York who said he was an engineer and had gotten his degree at Cornell. I was duly impressed since he seemed to be full of himself.

During the first couple of days, I found out that there were many of us second lieutenants recently arriving at Patrick that were not rated as pilots or navigators. Many were engineers who would be working at Cape Canaveral on the fledgling rocket program. Others were accountants, data processors, or management personnel who would be in supply or maintenance. It appeared to me that there was an abundance of young lieutenants that the Air Force had on its hands and was having a difficult time finding things for them to do.

As I was walking into the Officers Club for lunch another young lieutenant came up to me and saluted. I told him to forget the salute because I had just entered service two days ago.

It did not take me long to make many good friends and know co-workers who had recently come to Patrick. Many who were working at the Cape related that the future space program had gotten off to a good start and they were firing old V-II German rockets down range toward the islands in the Caribbean. The Atlas, Minuteman, and other space vehicles were still on the drawing boards or had not been dreamed up yet. I thought to myself what a great place to start my career, even though I didn't think that I would be in the Air Force for over two or three years.

I settled in at the BOQ and awaited Nancy and Jan who would arrive in May, when I obtained quarters either on the base or in a nearby town. On weekends Lt. Jack Noble and I took trips to Tampa, Silver Springs, Daytona Beach, Marineland, and St. Augustine so I got to see a lot of Florida. Six of us drove down to Palm Beach and chartered a fishing boat at Stuart for the day. We caught all kinds of fish and had a great time.

Ken Hill who served with me at Patrick and in Germany, after reading this chapter added, "Lt. Jack Noble (a civil engineer) was a bachelor and one of six that rented a house on the beach. The Master Bedroom had a sign on the door--In Use/ Not In Use!!"

Several young ladies traveling through Florida on their way to the southern coasts often dropped in at this and other bachelor beach houses in the area.

Nancy and Jan flew down in May and we moved into an apartment about 10 miles from the base in Eau Gallie across Indian River on the mainland. We lived in a building that had four units and ours was on the second floor. Since we had no air conditioning, Nancy who was five months pregnant and our year old Jan had to contend with the heat and mosquitoes. The double bed had a spring poking out and we had to get a sheet of plywood to make it firm enough. We had a difficult time getting the plywood home as Nancy and I had to hold it on the roof of our car for about five miles.

I had purchased a 1946 Pontiac about the time Nancy arrived. It had been on the coast for nine years and was nothing but rust. I had to replace two or three freeze plugs on the side of the engine block because they rusted. So, water would leak out and the engine would overheat. I bought the piece of junk for $200 and would not drive it anywhere except to the base and back. Nancy, with Jan and newborn Mike, drove it over the causeway to Highway A-1-A one morning. When they got there the brakes failed and they roared across the highway and ended up in a sand dune just above the beach. Also, I tried to repair a fuel pump, but found out that I was not much of a mechanic. A year later when we got orders to transfer, I sold the heap to a fellow for $100. He checked the rear bumper to see if he could put a trailer hitch on it because he said he intended to drive the car and a trailer to Maine. I have no idea if he made it or not.

The Comptroller, Colonel Robert Alston, decided that his three second lieutenants assigned to the accounting office should form a nonappropriated central accounting office and take care of the Officers Club, Noncommissioned Officers (NCO) Club and other small club activities on the base. I was assigned to keep the Officers Club books; Paul Vigianno the NCO Club books; and Marvin Loskove all the small club books. We had to post all activity to the ledgers each day, maintain a general ledger, oversee monthly inventories of liquors and food, and prepare monthly financial reports. The work was not difficult but it usually kept us busy. This was the first office of this type in the Air Force.

I got along great with Paul and Marvin. Paul was from New York and Marvin was from Memphis. After service, Paul returned to New York, got his law degree, and changed his name to Paul Victor. He worked as a prosecutor for the NYC District Attorney Office. Marvin returned to Memphis and worked for a CPA firm. Over the years, I lost contact with both of them but have always wished them the best.

We had a Captain Kenneth Gaither as our immediate supervisor who we didn't get along with very well. I don't know what his problem was but he gave the three of us mediocre Officer Effectiveness Reports (OERs). I had three and the last one rated me as a dependable and typically effective officer. Col. Alston who did not agree with Captain Gaither's rating upgraded my OER to "A very fine officer of great value to the service." Col. Alston's belief in me was the main reason that I was selected for a regular commission that I obtained a year later.

As the months passed, I liked service life more and more. It was much like college life, I didn't have a lot of responsibility and the friendships Nancy and I had with the other young families have lasted for years. Marilyn and Ed Kimball, Jo and Burke Bero, and Becky and Jim Jordan have remained close for over 50 years. We see Ed and Marilyn almost every year since they live in Cincinnati. We have visited Jo and Burke at their Cape Cod home and communicate with the Jordans who live in Florida.

In the middle of December, Nancy went home by train for Christmas with Jan and newborn Mike. Ed and Marilyn were going to Ohio for Christmas so I went with them in their old Buick. I think Ed slept most of the way to Kentucky and back so I ended up driving about 90% of the time. After Christmas, all of us hopped in the Buick and headed south. At four A.M. on a Sunday morning the car's lights started dimming about ten miles north of Tifton, Ga. We followed a car into town to the nearest filling station. The owner was good enough to take all of us and the babies in while he replaced the brushes in the generator. To make things worse, I backed up against a pot-bellied stove and burnt a hole in my new wool pants. After we got back in the car we motored on down to Patrick. Since there were no interstate highways at that time I think the trip from Lexington, Ky. with the stop in Tifton took 25 hours.

Nancy's living conditions in Eau Gallie were very hectic, especially as she was pregnant with Mike. Our apartment was hot, she had to throw a sheet over her head when she hung the wash on the clothes line because the mosquitoes were big enough to almost carry you away. Plus, Jan was a hand full, since she just passed her first birthday when they moved to Florida. Every morning during the summer an old bi-plane sprayed DDT just outside our bedroom window. The noise was a wake up call and I don't know if it made any difference in the mosquitoes or not since swarms still stuck around after the plane had flown by.

Even with all the inconveniences, we had a great time with our friends and things to do in Florida. The beach behind the Club was great, and only a few months after Mike was born he kept inching down to the water. He loved it. On the bridge over Indian River we spent many nights with a gasoline lantern and a net on a long pole catching shrimp. We caught a lot of angel fish there too. We purchased our first TV from the Kimballs and Jan started watching Captain Kangaroo and the Mickey Mouse Club. We spent many late evenings watching the Tonight Show with Steve Allen and his gang, and followed the rise of Elvis Presley. Nancy's family came down and spent a few days. I don't think Linda and Hugh cared about the heat and sleeping on the apartment floor because of the roaches. All in all, this was one of the favorite times of our life.

On October 3, 1955, Mike arrived in the world. We lived about 10 miles from the base and had to drive over a drawbridge to get to the base hospital. Around 1:00 A.M., Nancy woke me up and told me that the time had come and we should get to the hospital. In a very few minutes we had a baby sitter for Jan and I was ready to go but Nancy piddled around until I told her to forget the chores and lets go. She reluctantly relented so we took off in our old crate. We didn't have to wait for the draw bridge since no boats were out that early in the morning. We pulled into the hospital and I took her to admissions and went back to park the car. Two minutes later, I returned and found Nancy in the delivery room and Mike had arrived.

Nancy's mother Jessie arrived and helped out after Nancy came home. We didn't have a washer, so Jessie told us to go to Sears in Orlando and get one. After that we threw the old wash board away. When Jessie left, my Mom came down and spent some time with us. She was very helpful, but when she left we were glad to be alone with our babies.

We played cards and shared dinners with our friends, the Kimballs, Beros and Jordans. The Kimballs came over from their quarters at the base near the coast and spent the night when a major hurricane blew by heading north about 100 miles east of the coast. Nancy's friend Libba Harris came and spent a week with us as did Nancy's sister Linda and her friend. One of the lieutenants spied Linda at the officers club and later visited her in Nashville. Even though we lived on a meager salary we truly enjoyed Air Force life. I decided to apply for a regular commission and stay in until retirement 20 or 30 years in the future.

I continued to play basketball and several of my buddies were my teammates on the officer club and base teams. While traveling with the base team I experienced my first occurrence of racial discrimination. We had a black player traveling with us who could not get served in a small restaurant in central Florida. This opened my eyes to the problems blacks had in the south, and the experience remained with me the rest of my life.

During the season, Bobby "Goose" Brown a buddy and great player on U of L's basketball team came to Patrick with the Tyndall AFB team to play us. I had a good game and actually scored one basket when he was guarding me. He spent the next day with Nancy and me, so we showed him the sights, such as they were, and fed him a meal before he left.

At the end of the season, our team flew up to Panama City, Fl. and played in a tournament. I usually was the second string center, but our starter at that position did not make the trip. We arrived late in the afternoon and many of us hit the officers club for dinner and drinks. I drank too many sweet whiskey sours that made me sick. The next morning at 9 A.M. we had our first game. Even though I felt the effects of the night before, I had the best game I ever had. Burke Bero kept feeding me the ball and I scored 31 points while missing 10 or more free throws. We played two additional games before we were eliminated and I played well in each of those.

After I applied for the regular commission, I received orders in late summer of 1956 to transfer to Germany in the fall. I was elated but most of the family questioned our family going overseas for the next three years. On August 29, I put on my silver bars as a first lieutenant and knew that I had made the right choice to stay in the Air Force. In October, we left Patrick and took 30 days leave prior to being assigned to the 317th Troop Carrier Wing, Neubiberg AB, Germany with a reporting date of November 9, 1956. On the last evening at Patrick, we had dinner at the Kimballs. On our way out their door we heard the rattle of a rattle snake in the bushes in front of the Kimball's house. We all jumped in the car, headed to our apartment, spent the night and got on the train the next day to Tennessee where we visited the folks in Nashville, Harrodsburg, and Louisville.

My leave flew by and I left Louisville by train to New York for my flight to Germany. I hated to go because I knew that Nancy and the kids would have to wait 4 to 6 months before I got family living quarters there.

Neubiberg AB, Munich, Germany - 11/56 - 2/58

I departed Louisville on the train and had a compartment from Cincinnati to New York. I quartered at the Brooklyn Navy Yard and spent a couple of days processing and sightseeing in Times Square via the subway. After a bus ride from the city, I boarded a USAF DC - 6 at McGuire AFB. The four engine prop driven plane had refueling stops in Newfoundland and Amsterdam, Holland before arriving at Rhein Main AFB, Frankfurt, Germany, 18 to 20 hours after leaving the USA. The flight was uneventful except when the auto pilot malfunctioned and the plane dropped a few hundred feet in a split second. I was belted in but the fellow beside me and a few others were thrown from their seats. I remember that I read the novel "No Time For Sergeants" during the long flight when I wasn't looking out the window watching oil leak out of the engines onto the wing.

I spent the night at Rhein Main and caught the train to Munich the next day. When I arrived in Munich, I obtained military transportation to Neubiberg AB located on the outskirts of the city just off the Autobahn (expressway). I immediately processed in and reported to the comptroller, Major Elwood Hintz. He told me I would be the 317th Troop Carrier Wing accounting officer and would have a staff of several military, U. S. civil service, and German national personnel. I did not know what I was getting into since I had not had this amount of responsibility before.

A US civil service lady was in charge of appropriation accounting and her husband was the budget officer. They knew what they were doing but did not teach me the basics of their responsibilities. I had a chief master sergeant as my assistant and he taught me what was needed to maintain appropriation accounting records when the two above civilians took leave for a month back to the States. The sergeant and I burned the midnight oil balancing the books and preparing monthly reports to our major command, Hq.USAFE (United States Air Forces in Europe). It was critical that I learn this system because I had to sign and certify that we had funds available to pay for the items noted on obligation documents, i.e. supplies, services, travel, civilian pay, etc. If there were not available funds and I signed documents saying there were, I could have broken Federal regulation (AF Reg 177-16) and faced court marshal proceedings or other punishment. Needless to say, I learned my duties very quickly.

On April 11, 1955, I changed my serial number from AO3032778 to FR 31762, the effective date that I was accepted into the regular air force. At that time I really felt that I belonged and intended to remain in service until I retired.

For six months I lived in the BOQ, since Nancy, Jan and Mike would not be allowed to come to Germany until I was provided government quarters. I played basketball on the squadron and base teams and the most notable thing that occurred was a team trip to Ulm where we played an Army team. At half time, Don Purcell came into the locker room and said when he saw my skinny legs he knew it was Buck Lively. Don had played football with me at U of L for two years. During the second half of that game I was ejected because I set too much of a pick (block) on an opponent. That was the first and only time I was ever thrown out of a game for rough play.

The Wing's mission was to fly and drop 11th Airborne troops on training missions all over free Europe. The pilots and navigators living in the BOQ were all young and many were wild. German girls from downtown bars clopped up and down the BOQ halls to the bath and shower rooms many of the nights. I stayed away from that activity but heard the details every now and then.

During my stay at Neuibiberg my office had a party downtown at the Octoberfest (a huge beer fest in downtown Munich) and several of us attended Fasching parties in Munich's hotels and the House Der Kunst Museum. These events were similar to New Orleans Marde Gras celebrations for six weeks before Lent. A lot of the fellows spent much of their time in the Alps skiing. After seeing several come back in casts, I decided that my gimpy knee probably would not survive the slopes.

We never lost any aircraft or crews while there, but I heard enough tales to know that we were lucky we didn't. A buddy, Bob Bennett, who later was one of the first persons killed in Viet Nam, wanted me and a couple of other fellows to fly with him to England over a weekend in a B-26. I couldn't go because of a basketball game. When he returned he said he had a fire in the plane's cabin and while trying to put it out both engines stopped because the reserve fuel tanks had not been switched on while he was fighting the fire. He got the fire extinguished and the engines restarted and then had an uneventful flight back to Neuibiberg.

Later, I went up with him to fly around the area. We flew on one engine, skimmed low over a lake near Munich buzzing the sailboats, and made touch and go landings and takeoffs. While doing this the cockpit canopy broke loose from its latches but did not come completely open because Bob had tied a strap around the latch. He told me to hold the canopy together until we landed. He wrote the problem up, but the latch was not repaired and later someone on a two hour flight had it happen again and the entire hatch blew out. Thus, he had a "convertible" for an hour or so until he reached the base.

The pilots in the C-119s flew low over the fields in Turkey and scattered sheep. In one instance a pilot was flying in the valleys of Turkish mountains when he came upon a mountain right in front of him. He did a 180 degree turn and those in the plane said he knocked rocks off the mountains all through the turn. In another instance a C-119 pilot lost an engine halfway across the Mediterranean sea. The crew threw everything out to reduce weight and just made it back to Italy.

Nancy and the kids got orders to come to Germany in April 1956. Nancy's mother, Jessie Dorsey, accompanied them on the train to New York. As soon as they arrived Nancy went to the processing station where they told her that a slot had come open on the America. If she wanted to go by sea she could, but would have to hurry to the dock because the ship was scheduled to sail in only a couple of hours. Nancy asked what the America was and they told her it was the sister ship of the liner United States, and she and the children would sail first class. She decided that she would take the ship instead of flying. She made it to the ship on time and left her mother standing on the dock as she and the kids sailed off. Jessie immediately returned to the train station and took the first train back to Tennessee.

The voyage to Bremerhaven, Germany lasted eight days and Nancy enjoyed it very much even though she had two small children with her. The ship's crew made sure that she was well taken care of. She liked the voyage so much that she wanted to be sure that we sailed home at the end of our tour.

In Bremerhaven, Nancy boarded a military train to Munich. She had two small compartments. When the German military personnel on the train tramped past her door in their heavy boots, Nancy locked her compartment's door because she had seen too many war movies about Nazi Germany. One German man wanted to give Jan a glass of beer, but Nancy politely refused because Jan was only three years old.

The arrival in Munich's train station was a joyous event and I took the family to our new home in the Ramersdorf military housing complex in southeast Munich. The complex had numerous three story apartment buildings located about five miles from the base. Our two bedroom apartment was located on the second floor. It was completely furnished with china, crystal, and silverware and anything one would need. I hired a maid, Margaret, who was a jewel. Three days a week she came in the morning, cleaned the house, and stayed until dinner was over. She was great and loved little Mikey, who she placed on her back when she waxed the floors on her knees.

We made many friends and enjoyed the friendship of Jack and Kathryn Rash, Ken and Trelle Beckner, Floyd and Earlene Jack, bachelors living in the BOQ, and many others. We had good times at the Club, outings at Garmish, Tegernsee, Munich restaurants, and family drives in our old Opel sedan. We took a drive to Dauchau concentration camp and saw the barracks and ovens where the Nazis killed thousands of innocent people.

After a wedding reception one evening, we returned to our apartment. Later, Nancy looked out of the window and saw our old Opel going down the street. A couple of German kids stole, took a joy ride, and wrecked it.. We didn't get any restitution, so I salvaged a radio and had it junked. A few days later I bought an old hard top Mercury that I drove until I transferred back to the States.

About six months after Nancy arrived we met Ken and Betsy Hill at the Club one evening. We learned that they lived behind the Kimball's at Patrick. They became our close friends and we later lived near them in Wiesbaden, Germany and Alexandria, Va.

Halfway through my assignment, we had a change of command. The new commander, Col. Henry J. Amon, was quite an individual. He made full colonel during World War II and never made general. He had the longest tenure in grade than anyone in the service. His reputation for squirrely actions were well known. One pilot stopped at Neubiberg for the night and saw Col. Amon's picture on the wall. He decided to fly on to another base because he didn't want to be on the same base with him. Col. Amon would direct traffic in the Base Exchange parking lot and would have a car towed in because it was on the line of his private parking place in the Club's parking lot. He called a sergeant on the carpet because the sergeant's child did not know who Col. Amon was when Amon asked the child if he knew his name. He would not turn in a guard dog assigned to him when he left Neubiberg to go to his new assignment at Rhein Main. Lastly, he had some furniture put on a plane back to the States. This was a questionable practice because the weight allowance on moving furniture to and from Germany was four thousand pounds. The pilot off loaded the furniture in the Azores. I don't know how he got it back the rest of the way.

During the spring of 1957, we learned that the troop carrier wing was going to be moving to France and Neubiberg AB would be returned to the German government. With this change I had to fly over to Evereux AB, France to do some work in the transfer. After three days there and one evening in Paris with some of my buddies from Neubiberg, now stationed in France, I had to catch a flight back to Neubiberg. Ken Beckner and his crew picked me up and let me sit in the jump seat behind the pilot and copilot. We had to abort on takeoff because the copilot was swerving off the runway. We made another stop in France to pick up some cargo, but was cut off in our final approach by a couple of fighters in a hurry to get on the ground. After picking up the cargo, we headed across the Alps to a base in Aviano, Italy. Ken had let me sit in the copilot seat and I had the controls just as we were halfway across the Alps. At that exact time a fire warning light lit up on the instrument panel. Thank goodness that it was a malfunctioning light, because I would have hated to parachute into the Alps below. After that, the flight ran smoothly.

It looked like I would be transferred to France, but someone at the 7100 Support Wing in Wiesbaden must have liked my work and requested that I be sent there. Early in 1958, I received orders to move to Wiesbaden. Nancy and the children would have to stay in Munich for a few weeks until I was assigned living quarters in Wiesbaden. On February 13, 1958, I left Munich for Wiesbaden.

Lindsey Air Force Station, Wiesbaden 2/58-10/59

Upon arriving at Wiesbaden, I was told that I would be in charge of the Command Fiscal Station, located at Lindsey Air Station in downtown Wiesbaden, the home of HQ. USAFE. The Command Fiscal Station reported to the comptroller of the 7100th Support Wing located at Wiesbaden Air Force Base. Wiesbaden AFB performed all supporting duties for HQ. USAFE. Thus, I had to serve two superiors. If I kept the USAFE brass happy, my bosses at the AFB would leave me alone.

About a month after I arrived, two auditors dropped in to audit the operations I was responsible for. The lead auditor was Warrant Officer Ralph Albert Capone who I would serve with in the U. S. Department of Agriculture several years later. He became one of my best friends. I told Al to find everything that he could that was wrong because I had just arrived and would do all that I could to correct noted discrepancies. Needless to say they found plenty.

I had a staff of about 20 military, U.S. civilian and German nationals. They performed accounting duties including maintaining general ledger and cash flow appropriation records and preparing monthly, quarterly and annual reports,

To put it briefly, we were allotted funds in about ten different accounts, and had to maintain "checkbook" entries in each of these accounts on millions of dollars of expenditures annually. This was done after converting many foreign currencies into US dollars or German marks. We also had the responsibility of allotting funds to every USAFE Air Base to cover dependent school teachers salaries and travel costs. Each base would report to us each month their expenditures and the balances in their accounts. We would consolidate these figures in our reports to higher headquarters monthly. To make matters worse USAFE budget office expected to use all or at least 99 percent of the funds allotted each year so that the next years budget would not be reduced.

At the end of the fiscal year, June 30th, there would be a push to use all the money allotted. At eleven PM on one June 30th, I received a desperate call from the budget officer to see if I had available funds they could take from me to transfer to another station for an expenditure they could make. I was able to transfer over $100,000 that was "hidden" for such an occurrence.

Once an accounting officer from an AFB in England called and said that he thought he had an over obligation in his school funds. I told him not to worry that we had sufficient funds and would cover him by back dating a transfer of funds to his account. This covered him and negated any costly investigation or penalty of violating AF Reg 177-16. One time, one of my German accountants confused French Francs for Belgium Francs, and we almost had a violation. However, we found enough "hidden" funds that were not in use to correct the mistake.

USAFE budget called me one day after the end of the fiscal year and said that someone at another base had purchased a fire truck in the prior year without having approved funding. They would get me the money in the prior year funds to purchase the truck. The purchase order I signed showing that money was available for the truck had been previously requested, approved, and signed by two Generals.

During my couple of years at the Command Fiscal Station, I had to juggle funds from one account to another almost daily. Before I signed anything expending money I consulted my own private "checkbook accounts" to see if there were funds available because I didn't trust the official book balances.

About six months before I was to transfer back to the States, USAFE budget officials asked me to take a job with them because a civilian had died. I would have to extend my tour one year for this good opportunity. I turned it down because we needed to return to the States as Nancy's dad had passed away a few months earlier. When I transferred my replacement was a Major.

A couple of months after arriving at Wiesbaden, Nancy, Jan and Mike arrived and we had quarters in the Hainerburg housing area. The quarters were nice and we had good neighbors who became close friends. Ken and Betsy Hill and their two girls Nancy and Susan, arrived about the same time and lived near us. We learned to play bridge with the Hills and Ken introduced me to golf, which I truly enjoy but never improved much over the years. We would go out to the course early on foggy Saturday mornings and could not see 100 yards down the fairways, but managed to get in 18 holes before noon.

Nancy and Betsy were both pregnant and expecting within a week or so apart. The day before Len arrived we played bridge with the Hills all day and had waffles for dinner.

Nancy delivered Len the next morning at the Lindsey hospital. Betsy had Craig two weeks later. Both deliveries went well but Len was put in an incubator for a couple of days as precautionary measure because he had trouble breathing just after birth.

Floyd and Earline Jack and their four children also came to Wiesbaden from Neubiberg and lived in another complex of quarters a few miles away. John and Georgia Filhol and their children lived above us. John was from Monroe, La. and was an Air Police lieutenant. He related that he had the most difficult time getting Col Amon to give up the Air Force police dog assigned to him at Neuibiberg when he left for Rhein Main.

John was a good buddy who I respected a lot, and later visited in Louisiana. Raymond and Charlotte Frank lived in the next apartment building behind us. Raymond was with the Office of Investigation (OSI) and later became sheriff of Travis County (Austin), Texas since he had previously served L. B. Johnson. Raymond had two grandfather clocks that he had bought from some German families and he sold them to me just before we transferred back to the States. I still have one and Nancy's mother, Jessie, has the other one.

With our friends we had good times dining and dancing at the Von Steuben Military Hotel and the good restaurants in and around Wiesbaden. The Hills, Jacks, and Nancy and I took a Rhine River cruise lasting all day that was sponsored by the Officers Club. We took pictures of the castles and vineyards along the river banks and stopped at Bingen for lunch.

Ken Hill read a draft of this chapter and added the following.

"Floyd and Earline Jack had a knockout maid that entertained the guests on occasion. Floyd Jack drank French 75's at my house and picked up Bets and dropped her, when she was several months pregnant. Earline was a winner at five and dime poker.

Bill and Nancy --Ken and Bets took a Rhein River cruise to see castles on the Rhein. Ken jumped to boat no. 2 and could not offload to visit the castles. He was unfortunately trapped with the 12 German hostesses (Tough duty)!

Col Henry J Amon also had aboard the aircraft with his furniture a freezer of prime steaks from the Officers Club--after the club had a free Brunswick Stew nite!! and closed permanently.

The golf course was Rheinblith and had a hole that only Mt. goats could climb.

The downtown Von Steuben Hotel was atop a hill and Bets & I came all the way down on the ice in my VW (backwards) a few days after Xmas.

There were many good times at Neuibiberg and Wiesbaden and of course all the great trips. I think we made about the same ones that you mentioned, I had overall surveillance responsibilities for construction in Germany and France. With my job was blanket orders to visit any site in G. or F. I could drive my 57 Dodge sweep wing HT all over on 15cents/gallon gasoline!!"

Nancy's grandfather, Fay, came to see us during his tour of Europe. The Jacks had a party for him and gave him a knife as a remembrance. During his visit, we received word that his son, and Nancy's dad had died. Grandpa stayed with us and didn't go back home to the funeral. We were glad that he was with us at that time because he and Nancy comforted each other. Nancy could not go back anyway because she was six months pregnant

While at Wiesbaden, Floyd Jack and I took a weekend flight to Rome. While there I got to the Coliseum, the catacombs, and took a horse and buggy ride around the city. When I returned to the hotel I found Floyd sitting on the toilet drinking wine and soaking his feet in the bidet. Later, John Filhol and I took a weekend flight to Athens where we saw the Acropolis and stayed at a hotel on the coast. On our flight hone, we bounced into the Rome airport so hard that we had to go around to land again. A colonel sitting next to me had turned white and wondered if we had blown out a tire on the first bounce. Four hour per month pilots were sometimes scary to fly with.

Nancy and Charlotte Frank took a tour to Paris for three or four days by bus. I had to also go to Paris as well as Munich on business. I drove up to Brussels for the Worlds Fair and stayed one day. Later, Nancy, the kids and I drove to Holland and stayed on the beach at Scheveningen at a great hotel. We toured Amsterdam, the Hague, and Marken Island on the Zider Zee. On all these trips we made slides that we still see and recall all the good times of our past.

About two months before I transferred back to the States, I received word that I would be stationed at Scott Air Force Base, Illinois and would be assigned to the resident auditor's office as an auditor for the U. S. Air Force Auditor General organization. This would be the start of my auditing career that I cherished for all these years.

Just before we were ready to return home, Mom wrote and asked my permission to marry Jim Parsons. I replied that she was over 21 years old and could do what ever she wanted and, since she had dated this old bachelor before she married my dad, I wished her every happiness. A couple of weeks before we left I received a great letter from my brother Thomas, that I lost, telling me that he was proud of the person that I had become and wished that I would come back and work with him. As we were getting ready to leave we received word that Thomas had crashed in his plane in the fog while returning to Minneapolis from Denver. My sister went to the funeral which was held before I could get home.

We came home on the USS Randall, a Navy transport ship. The cruise from Bremerhaven to New York took an eventful eight days. Our cabin was on one of the top decks and as I looked out of the porthole I said I would become worried if the waves hit this high up. We sailed through the English channel and on a foggy morning we could barely see the white cliffs of Dover. After a couple of days in the North Atlantic we sailed through the tail end of a hurricane and the waves did hit our porthole. Almost everyone on the ship was sick except us because I had all the family eat as much as they could. Jan looked a little queasy but managed to stay OK. We arrived in New York and had to remain in the harbor overnight due to a lack of a berth at the port.. The Statue of Liberty and the New York skyline were beautiful after being away for three years.

The next day we took the train to Louisville and just before we were to arrive I dropped my partial plate down the sink. After much tinkering I was able to retrieve it and it was all in one piece. In Louisville we were met by all the family and Len saw all of his relatives for the first time.

CHAPTER 5

11/59 -- 3/65

Scott Air Force Base 11/59 - 1/62

After 30 days leave in Kentucky and Tennessee, we traveled to Scott AFB, in Belleville, Illinois which was about 25 miles east of St. Louis Missouri. We obtained quarters in base housing, an apartment with two bedrooms and one bath. I reported to the Resident Auditors office and met my commander, Major Edward Smithwick, a secretary, two civilian auditors, and three other military officers. The civilians were Elroy Wells and Charlie Walters. The military were Maj. Nordquest, and Lieutenants Annelli and Shields. Later Bob Storrs, another civilian joined our office. Everyone in the office got along fine and we had great relationships both during office and after duty hours.

Elroy was the deputy and reviewed most of the work papers and draft audit reports. He made a lot of editorial changes in the drafts. Some of which improved the reports and others were questionable. If you wrote in the active voice, he would change it to the passive, and would reverse it if you wrote in the passive voice This scrutiny helped me in years to come when trying to get reports approved and issued during my years with Agriculture. Everyone got used to this and didn't mind, if the intent was not changed.

During lunch hours, we would play a game of hearts, cribbage, and later liars dice. Jack Annelli became a great friend and we played on the squadron basketball team, as well as golf whenever we had a chance. He was from Massachusetts, went to Holy Cross and was an avid Boston Celtics basketball fan. We saw several games in St. Louis when Boston came to town and attended the NBA finals when Boston and St. Louis met in 1962. We also attended several St. Louis Cardinal baseball games as well as the pro St. Louis Cardinal football games.

Besides basketball, I coached and played on the squadron touch football team which won the base championship. In an all-star game involving officer vs. the airmen I intercepted a pass and ran it in for the winning touchdown. This was the first touchdown I ever scored in over six years of high school and college action.

During my stay at Scott, I learned what it took to become a proficient auditor. On my first assignment I misstated an amount in the audit report which the client caught during the exit conference. As a result we had to alter the final report and put in the correct figure. The next day Maj. Smithwick put a sign over my desk with the following quote "Be right before you write." This stuck with me during my years of auditing.

There are several things that one needs to become a good auditor. I will list them in the order that I feel is most important. Others may not feel what I have listed below applies.

1. Integrity--Every auditor should be beyond reproach. I have seen cases where this trait has been abused. Most of the time the auditor's lack of independence with the client resulted in unreported or watered down audit findings. The recent Enron/auditor relationships plus others are good examples of the lack of integrity on the auditors part. This happened more than once during my audit experience. Later passages in this biography will indicate what I feel as the lack of integrity by some of my co-workers.

2. Common Sense--All the technical knowledge a person may have may not be worth anything if this person does not use common sense. I have seen supervisors or auditors waste their time examining insignificant documents for hours on end. In other instances some auditors never used their creativity to develop methods to discover if management problems existed. Some reports contained frivolous findings that only served to

anger management. These are only a few of the instances where auditors did not use common sense.

3. Job Knowledge--An auditor needs to have the technical ability from education and experience to perform audits and must be able to use what tools are available to determine what is fact and what is fiction. He should use data processing and statistical sampling techniques to the fullest. It is amazing that in 2004 we have found that the FBI still uses outdated computers that one wonders if the agent in the field is capable of using.

4. Management of People, Time, and Resources--The greatest thing about managing people is the ability to delegate authority to the best extent possible. If an auditor has the responsibility to manage an assignment he must have the authority to make needed decisions, use available resources, and delegate authority to subordinates to successfully complete the mission. Management of time is critical to insure that needed audit coverage is completed in a timely manner (time is money!). The auditor should use all the resources that are available and needed to assure success.

5. Auditor/Client Relationship--Good relationships need to be maintained despite the need for independence. Tact with management is a must. Auditors are prone to "dig for the dirt" which is good if not carried to the extreme. Auditing is much like investigative reporting by the media. While important or critical findings may upset local management the government auditor has to realize that he is working for the citizens of the United States and must report such findings. Therefore it behooves the auditor to try to maintain good local relationships with management without infringing on the auditor's integrity.

6. Communication Skills--Oral and written communications must be clear, concise and contain needed contents without being verbose. Usually these skills come with experience. A properly prepared written report, briefing or audit result discussion will "grease the wheels" for agreements of all parties. These skills are also needed in relationships between subordinates and one's bosses. The need to communicate fully and honestly is a prerequisite for good employee/employer relationships.

There are many other things that are requirements for auditors but the above six are what I have found most important and the things I had to learn when I started my audit career at Scott AFB. A lot of times the use of common sense led to great creativity in performing audit tasks. Sometimes small insignificant items resulted in huge findings that had a profound impact on the audit if the auditor used his head and said "what if?" instead of bypassing this small concern.

During my family's two years at Scott, Jan and Mike began school close to our quarters and we made new friends with our neighbors in our apartment complex. Nancy and I played bridge and went into St. Louis for dinner quite often. Since we were close to Tennessee and Kentucky we made many trips home and our families visited us several times. The worst thing that happened to us was that Nancy lost our fourth child in her second month of pregnancy.

When we returned from Germany, Mom gave me her old Buick which we drove for almost a year. We traded it in for a new small Pontiac Tempest station wagon. We took a trip in the new car to Dallas, Texas and saw the Lichvars for a couple of days. I played golf with Bob, and Nancy had a good time with Evelyn. We left Dallas and drove to Oklahoma City to visit Uncle Frank and Aunt Jennie Lively. Although she had more money than she could ever spend, she collected junk pottery as well as nice things that were stacked on her dining room table. They took us to the local cafeteria to have lunch since there was little room for cooking in her house. After Oklahoma City, we returned to Scott.

About a week later a fellow who was late for work smashed into the front left side of my new car resulting in a lot of body work. Fortunately neither he nor I were hurt. I kept this car for about two more years and had problems with it most of the time.

On October 15, 1961, I was promoted to Captain and was happy to change from one silver bar on my shoulder to two. I had audited several different entities at Scott and the most important thing that I found was that the hospital had purchased several pagers for staff doctors costing $35,000 that were not on accountable records. The only time these pagers were used, since they were so cumbersome to carry around, was when the doctors played golf. We recommended that other hospitals within the command be sure that pagers would be used before purchasing additional ones.

General LeMay decided that Air Force supply units worldwide did not have good accountability over supply stocks so he ordered Project Count, a re-inventory of all stocks world wide. The inventory was taken and base auditors were required to verify the counts on a sample basis. I don't remember if inventories corrected many mistaken balances of items, but I remember we spent several days recounting small items like screws, nuts, etc.

One of the funniest things I remember that happened was when Lt. Shields decided to count all the fire extinguishers on the base. During his inventory he did not mark each extinguisher to insure that it had been counted. About halfway through his inventory he found out that he had counted the same extinguisher four or five times, because airmen moved them after he had counted them.

Another humorous occurrence involved a Captain, whose name I've forgotten. His family lived across the street from us and everything he did turned out disastrous. He had a high priced dog that he intended to use for breeding purposes. On taking a couple of weeks leave he boarded the dog with the vet.

Upon departure he told the vet to worm, wash and spray his dog. When the Captain returned he learned that his dog had been spayed instead of sprayed. A couple of months later this captain received notification that he would be transferred to Japan. He immediately went to the Cadillac dealer and purchased the largest limousine available, so that he could take it to Japan and sell it for a large profit. To his chagrin, his orders were changed to another base in the States soon after he took possession of the car.

Maj. Smithwick was replaced by Maj Bruce Gibson during the summer of 1961. About that time, I tried to move from a two bedroom quarters to a three bedroom one. Maj Gibson had not been able to get adequate quarters on base and had to move to a private residence off the post. I guess he felt that if he could not get adequate base housing then neither should I. So he prevented me from getting larger quarters for my three children. This upset me and I decided to request transfer to another base. I had heard good reports about the audit office in Memphis, Tenn. from a fellow who had been assigned there. Headquarters approved my request for transfer and early in January we moved to Memphis, Tennessee.

Memphis Resident Audit Office 1/62 - 7/63

The Memphis Resident Audit Office was supervised by Peter Moretta, a GS-13 civil service employee, three other civilians, Lt. Bill Flynn and me. It did not take me long to learn that Pete ran a "loose organization" since we went out to lunch all over town and occasionally played golf late in the afternoons. These little distractions did not detract from accomplishing our audits timely and efficiently. If someone needed to take a course such as computer applications and audit headquarters turned down the request, Pete would get the funding for the course from the Depot. As a result, our office was way ahead of others in using the computer to produce good audit results.

I greatly respected Pete, Charlie Palmer, George Hall and Bill Flynn. They were very good to be around and very qualified in performing audits. I learned much from them. In one audit they determined that spare parts for automobiles were purchased at the time the autos were obtained, but these parts were not used and became surplus. Dealers would purchase these used parts for 90% discounts then sell them back to the Government at full price. For example, the same automobile generator/alternator could be used for many years on new autos being produced yearly.

The most noteworthy audit that I performed pertained to the provisioning for the purchase of new crash/fire trucks that various commands needed in the coming year. Pete wrote in my annual effectiveness report the following, "He originated and effectively used a new audit approach to evaluate high cost equipment requirement computations. Results of his new technique and audit were: (1) duplicate requirement and authorizations were discovered that would have resulted in a $1.5 million excessive procurement of crash/fire trucks, (2) $8.4 million of crash/fire trucks assigned to ANG (Air National Guard) units were not used for their primary mission-support of operational aircraft … this condition could cause the $11.1 million of new ANG crash/fire truck requirement to be excessive. Operating personnel readily accepted his recommendation and took necessary action to correct requirement and authorization documents."

The family enjoyed Memphis since Nancy's sister Linda and new husband Billy Gaw were there. Bill was attending University of Tennessee Medical School. He was one of the most brilliant young men I have ever known. He finished high school at 16, college at 18, and Med. school at 22. He decided not to intern immediately, but went back to the eastern hills of Tennessee and practiced until he was called into the Army where he did his internship. After his Army tour he returned to Nashville and practiced in two hospital emergency rooms until he retired because of health problems.

Jan and Mike were in grade school about two blocks from our house in Whitehaven. We lived a couple of miles from Elvis Presley's mansion. Our first dog was given to us by Nancy's mother Jessie. Misty was a boxer and stayed in our backyard and house. She hated our neighbors dog, an Airedale, and would almost tear the door down to fight her. Her bad habit was to pass gas, then turn her head around and sniff, then get up and go into the next room.

Len ran around the house and yard with his blanket and thumb in his mouth. He had a little girl friend who owned the Airedale and also sucked her thumb. It was amusing to see them walking around the yard holding hands and sucking their thumbs.

The big national event at this time was the Cuban missile crisis. Jan and Mike spent several minutes in the school hall during atomic bomb warning tests. Everyone was considering building an underground bomb shelter. It was a tense time.

The other event of national interest involved the desegregation of the University of Mississippi by admitting James Meredith. Memphis was the staging point for the 11th and 82nd Airborne troops that were camped at the Air National Guard post within the perimeters of the Memphis Airport. I saw a lot of them encamped there because I was auditing the ANG operations at the time.

Our greatest event occurred on March 28, 1963, when Billy was born at Baptist Hospital. Eighteen days later, on April 15, his cousin and Linda's son Shannon was born. They have been very close ever since. When Billy came home from the hospital we wondered what our boxer Misty would think of him. Instead of being jealous that dog immediately took up residence under his crib and if he wasn't there she would go around the house looking for him.

We had a great time in Memphis, but the Auditor General thought it was time for me to move on to bigger and better things. They decided that I should become the resident auditor at another base and cut orders for me to transfer to Kincheloe AFB, Michigan effective July 2, 1963.

Kincheloe AFB 7/63-6/64/

We packed our belongings, got in our Pontiac Tempest and motored up to the northern peninsula of Michigan close to the town of Saulte Ste. Marie on the Canadian border. The base was an Air Defense Command Wing with squadrons of F-102 Delta Dart aircraft. It also had a SAC tenant of B-52 bombers. Both the ADC and SAC outfits were commanded by Colonels.

When we left Memphis the temperature was in the high 90s and when we arrived at Kincheloe it was in the low 30s and we had our coats on We were told that the seasons were July, August and Winter. We believed it. Later we found out what winter weather in upper Michigan was like.

I replaced a civilian as the resident auditor and there were three of us assigned to my office, a secretary who had lived in the upper peninsula all her life and Lt. Roy Newman. This was the first time I managed my own office since being an accounting officer in Wiesbaden. My nearest boss was in Columbus, Ohio. I was responsible for assigning audits to be done or doing them myself, reviewing audit work, workpapers, draft reports, discussing audit results with base officials, and signing and issuing the final finished reports. Columbus Headquarters would review our work after it was finished. Thus, I was trusted to prepare and issue audit reports that met auditing standards. It was good to know that my superiors had faith in me to do a good job.

I was at Kincheloe about a year and the most important thing I did was to audit a radar site in the northern part of lower Michigan. I found that on site maintenance of the large early warning radars had a serious supply problem. A new computer system installed permitted needed parts for the sight to be supplied in small quantities. I asked to see the number of emergency requisitions for the year and the prior year before the new computer system was installed. Records showed that about twenty emergency requisitions occurred in the prior year while over hundreds were processed in the current year. I asked how long it took to get an emergency requisition for stocks to be received. If it was a high priority item they had to fly the item in by helicopter and it may take four or five days. As a result, if the item was not on hand the entire radar site could be shut down because they needed a fifteen cent fuse. Immediately Hq. ADC took management action and the Auditor General developed an audit program to survey the seriousness of this situation at selected radar sites.

We later noted commissary sales store operation deficiencies, deficiencies in the base communication activity, and an improper concessionaire contract for operating the Officer Open Mess. During a regional audit meeting in Columbus, Ohio, General George Brown awarded me the Air Force Commendation Medal for my work in Memphis.

We finished an audit of SACs maintenance activity and just before I left for the audit exit discussion with the Wing Commander, Nancy called and said a bulletin came over the television that President John F. Kennedy had been shot. We held our meeting even though all of us were in shock. As a result the base went on high alert and little other activity resulted until after the three day period when he was buried. Everyone was walking around in shock and wondering what would become of the country because we had lost a great leader.

Upper Michigan was a beautiful place to live. There were so many things to see across the border in Canada; the parks and waterfalls within easy driving distance; the Soo locks where huge iron ore ships exited Lake Superior to Lake Huron; Mackinac Island with its shops, carriage rides, and Grand Hotel; and the historic US and Canadian Saulte Ste Marie cities. My mother and Jim visited us a couple of times and Nancy's mother came up and she and I rode a tandem bicycle down the streets of Mackinac during a visit there.

We had over a hundred inches of snow during the winter. The snow started on the November day John Kennedy was shot and the next time we saw snowless ground was sometime in April. Every car had its radio antenna extended to the fullest with a red flag on it so it could be seen around corners because of snowbanks piled up from scraping the snow. My secretary said the worst snow that she had seen was when the electric and telephone lines were dragging in the snow drifts.

One day the snow had piled up in front of our door so we had to go through the window to get outside and shovel the snow away from our front door. Another time Mike came in and said he had lost a boot when he was jumping off a pile of snow that turned out to be a station wagon. I went out to look for it and I also mistakenly climbed on the snowdrift covering the station wagon.

Every day snowplows would fill our driveway with snow that we had to shovel out only to have it piled up again when the snowplow came back along our street. For all the snow our kids did not miss a day of school and the main roads were always clear.

Nancy loved it up there and it is one of her favorite places. We have returned a couple of times to visit all the places that we were so fond of. All the family enjoyed the area but on my next assignment I hoped to be stationed at a warmer place. For the months of December, January and February I don't think we had three days where the temperature rose above zero degrees. I got tired of shoveling snow and walking around in boots and parkas.

I felt that I should continue my education so I was selected for the a course from the Air Force Institute of Technology with studies at Michigan State University. I took an entrance test at Kincheloe and learned that I had been selected. Orders were cut and I was to report in June 1964.

Michigan State University 6/64 - 1/65

Upon reaching MSU and obtaining a house to live in, I was told that my entrance test scores were not very high and I would be a probationary student. Prior probationary students had been placed in classes with their contemporary Air Force officers. These probationary students had master degree classes and were included in study groups with their AF classmates.

I learned from a University official that they were trying something new. So unlike past probationary students I would not be allowed to enter the masters program but would have to take one academic quarter of undergraduate senior 400 level classes and maintain a 3.00 or better grade point average before I would be allowed to enter Graduate School. This was quite a shock, but since I was already on campus and had no other alternative I agreed to take the undergraduate courses. I knew that at Louisville ten years earlier I was not a great student and had a cumulative four year 2.50 grade point average. Thus, I knew that I would have a hard time achieving the 3.00 average.

I signed up for four classes in advanced accounting, money and capital markets, and computer programming. I really enjoyed the money and capital markets class and busted my butt studying for the other courses. I felt alone on an island while I was there and felt my ship was sinking and I had no life jacket. My Air Force friends were doing fine in their study groups and I think all of them passed with flying colors. Major Neil Meurlin, my close friend, told me later that if I had been put in with the rest of them I would have had no trouble. Maybe so, who knows.

At the end of the school quarter, my grades were two Bs and two Cs. Exactly the same 2.50 grade point average I had maintained at Louisville. Thus, since I did not obtain a 3.00, I was not admitted to the MBA program.

I felt and continue to feel that every hard time in ones life contributes to better things ahead. I prayed a lot at the time and asked God to give me a little bit of Solomon's wisdom. Nancy was with me all the way during this period and with her support and love I knew that I could weather the storm.

The children enjoyed their stay in Lansing. After an ice storm Jan and Mike put on their ice skates as soon as they got outside the front door and skated down the sidewalk until they reached a small ice rink in the school yard. Len had his tonsils out while there and Billy was a happy two year old.

We took a long leave and visited my folks in Ft. Myers Florida. After returning to Michigan, I received orders to report to the audit office at Wheelus AB, Libya. Little did I know what was ahead for my family and me.

CHAPTER 6

1965 -1967

Wheelus AB Tripoli, Libya

Flying eastward during the hours of darkness on March 16th passed quickly. We had a refuel stop at Shannon, Ireland at 4:00 A.M. St. Patrick's Day, so a couple of us had a green beer while there. Daylight broke early on the spring morning as I gazed out of the window of the DC-8.The sun in the southeastern sky lit up the snow capped Alps fifty or so miles away from the Mediterranean and the view from 35,000 feet was one that I'll never forget. We were less than an hour away from touchdown at Wheelus AFB, Tripoli, Libya, and every minute we flew southeastward was one more minute I would be away from civilization.

As we flew over the Mediterranean Sea, I wondered what my new assignment would be like. Soon I caught sight of the coast of North Africa. It looked like a great mass of sand jutting out into the beautiful blue Mediterranean.

Shortly, we began our descent over the east-west main runway at Wheelus. The city of Tripoli was about four miles west of the base. From the air, I got my first look at my new home for the next three years. The Mediterranean bordered the base on the north and a twelve foot concrete block wall encircled the other three sides. Later, I learned the wall extended for about seven miles and every inch of the top of it contained embedded broken pieces of glass. As we circled for our final approach, I noticed that there was very little green anywhere down there. And, as we touched down I could see the walls in the distance and felt like we had just landed in a great big sandbox.

It was about ten A.M. when I stepped off the "Freedom Bird" onto the hot sands of Wheelus Air Base. The surroundings were something else. Air Force personnel and their families were cluttered all over the passenger off loading area. All had smug smirks on their faces because they knew that the poor souls arriving had longer to stay at Wheelus than they. I soon found out that meeting the monthly "Freedom Bird" was a must for those fortunate enough to be returning Stateside soon.

Out of the crowd stepped a stringbean lieutenant with and elfish grin on his face. When he opened his mouth and introduced himself as Frank Nusspickle, I knew at once that he was a New Yorker. He helped me with my two B-4 bags to his ten year old black and white Buick which must have spent it's entire life in Libya. It had globs of mud all over it the size of softballs and when we pitched the bags in, the old crate bounced up and down like a yo-yo. I asked Frank about the globs of mud on old Betsy and he replied that there recently had been a ghibli and in the middle of it a storm occurred. Since I was still confused, Frank continued that a ghibli occurred when the wind shifted from the nearby Mediterranean to a northerly direction. Since the Sahara desert was only a couple of miles away hot ghibli winds carried large amounts of sand and dust in them. When it rained at the same time, mud showers occurred. It dawned on me at that moment, I had fallen in love with Wheelus. Frank took me for a ride around the base and showed me the main points of interest: the Movies, the Officers' Club, Cafeterias, Snack Bars, and the Base Exchange. We ended up at the Resident Audit Office where I met Major Tom Swole and his staff. Later Frank took me to the BOQ(Bachelor Officer Quarters) that would be my home until my family arrived. Because of the ten hour jet lag, I decided to hit the sack right away that Friday afternoon and slept in late on Saturday.

When I awoke, Lt. Jerry Solecki, an auditor who lived just down the hall from me came in and said that I had missed a good St. Patty's party Friday night. When I replied that I was sorry to have missed it but had the opportunity to have a green beer during our refueling stop in Shannon at 4:00 A.M. on

St. Patty's day, Jerry responded that some of the guys in the next BOQ had a Christmas tree up and would celebrate an early Christmas that evening.

Later that afternoon Jerry and I went to the Officers Club. As I stared at two Libyan bartenders, each with crossed eyes, I surmised that I had three years to stay at beloved Wheelus and took some time to calculate I had 94.6 million seconds left before I could jump on the Freedom Bird back to the States. Nancy and our four kids would be joining me sometime in June so I had to live the bachelors life in the BOQ for about three months.

The nickel/dime poker games and impromptu parties helped the off duty hours pass fairly smoothly. I settled in at work and met several characters who played major roles during my stay at Wheelus. These friends, co-workers and a few adversaries remain unforgettable and their support, closeness and sometimes confrontations had great impact on me in the years to come. The auditors were the most interesting people I have ever met. Each was very competent and had the desire to excel in any assignment. However, their personalities were as different as night and day. I found audit office personnel can be compared to the characters who played in the TV series "Barney Miller." The work would be accomplished efficiently while the atmosphere in the office was more like a circus.

When I arrived Major Swole was the Resident Auditor whom I replaced about five months after my arrival. Tom was a huge likable guy who had a well known talent for causing problems for both our Auditor General Headquarters, in Frankfurt, Germany as well as the Wheelus Command. He was the only person in the history of Wheelus who could think up enough excuses to return to the States. He had already been home three times in less than a year. His entire tour lasted only one year instead of the required eighteen month unaccompanied one. The Auditor General officials headquartered in Germany got tired of putting out the fires that Tom stirred up and decided to transfer him back to the States

Tom loved to cook in his BOQ room even though this was unauthorized. It caused a great deal of concern to base officials when feathers he plucked from four chickens stopped up his shower stall drain. He was quite overweight (270+), so he went on a high protein, low carbohydrate diet which included drinking two glasses of vegetable oil every day for a month. This concoction finally about did him in so he had to go to the hospital. Some of the medics felt that he might die. He survived, but after all that his weight jumped up an additional ten pounds. Besides cooking and eating, Tom was known to drink a little and his favorite scotch whiskey was Grants. He was a devout Catholic, and more than once after he had a few, he would start worrying about his chaplain drinking buddy. He felt Father Daly got too familiar with the nurses that frequented the BOQ parties. From my observations, Tom had nothing to worry about because Father Daly was a fun loving person.

One Saturday night Frank Nusspickle and his young bride Jo Anne had a party at their villa in the village of Sukel Juma. During the festivities Jo Anne decided to show the visiting ladies her new home.. When she opened the bathroom door, there sat big Tom asleep on the john with his pants down to his ankles and a glass of Grants sitting on the floor beside him. According to many this was the highlight of the evening; however, I suspect that Jo Anne had other thoughts.

Tom hated being separated from his wife and six kids, so he wrote and issued an audit report concerning political favoritism at Wheelus. The report was so controversial that Headquarters decided to transfer Tom back to the States. Thus, Tom got exactly what he wanted because he was reassigned to Myrtle Beach AFB, South Carolina with his wife and family. An enlisted man on leave in the States later told me that he saw Tom at Charleston, S. C. airport lugging a container containing four quarts of Grants. I bet one of them was three fourths empty.

After Tom left I was appointed Resident Auditor, and in a few weeks I realized how much I appreciated him. The best thing he did for me was to work a deal where I could return home and accompany my family to Libya. He left the office in good shape, the staff was well trained, and I did not have to change the mode of operations.

The return to the States to get the family was uneventful as I flew in to Charleston. Nancy didn't know that I had made the trip and I was going to walk in her mother's house and surprise her. However, I had a delay in Atlanta and decided to call her. I was going to take a weeks leave, but after I arrived we had a screw up in Nancy and the kid's passport. It was misrouted and took three weeks to arrive at Jessie's house. Thus, I used a months worth of leave and would be in the hole in leave time accrued. Our return to Wheelus went about as expected except that Len became lost in the Shannon, Ireland airport at the time our plane "the Freedom Bird" was supposed to takeoff. He came out of the restroom a few minutes before we had to leave. Nancy wrote her mother the following letter a few days after our Wheelus arrival but did not mention the Leonard episode.

"Dearest Mother,

Well here we are, and I know you must think us terrible for not getting that wire off sooner. Now I know why Bill didn't send me one any sooner than he did. There is so much confusion and business to take care of, and we're so tired that every time that we remembered to send it, it was too late (wires only go out in the mornings) so anyway, please forgive the long delay.

There's so much to tell you that I guess I'll start in the beginning. The plane was late getting to Charleston so we didn't leave until 11:20. We flew right up the coast so saw many cities lit up which was beautiful. From N. Y. we went to Newfoundland and then across. It became daybreak at 2 A.M. so it was a short night. We arrived at Shannon at 6:30 and were there for an hour and then it took only 3 1/2 hours to get to Tripoli. Coming from Ireland we crossed France, near Paris, the Riviera, the Alps, the Elbe, and Sicily. The whole flight was smooth (a few bumps here & there) the weather clear with quite a bit of cloud cover & haze at times but on the whole it was absolutely beautiful and I thoroughly enjoyed every bit of it - even though I still don't care much about being so far off the ground! (33,000 ft. it was). I'll certainly never forget how beautiful everything looked from up there. The flight was exactly 12 hours as we arrived here at 11:20 A.M. (Here it was 6:20 P.M.).

We really had a big reception - everyone from the office and all of Bill's BOQ buddies were there. Actually it was rather confusing, but fun. One of the fellows brought us to our rooms & another brought our luggage. After that we got some hamburgers & cokes and then just collapsed & slept.

The children were real troopers the whole time. They were so fascinated by it all. Billy got tired of it about an hour & a half out and got cranky so I gave him his "sleeping potion" and he slept until we got to Shannon then got back up and played all around the airport and then went back to sleep on the flight here so he certainly wasn't any problem. Thank goodness for that little suppository! Len slept both before & after Shannon, Mike slept a little before and that Jan, she didn't go to sleep until an hour before we got here and when she got off the plane she burst into tears - she was absolutely exhausted. Boy, has the time change ever gotten hold of us - the first day went along fine but the second night & last night -wow- the two little ones went to sleep about 10 - Jan & Mike not at all, then about 2 A.M. everybody woke up - we had a parade to the bathroom, much chatter, & finally to sleep & stay asleep until late in the day - yesterday it was 1 o'clock before we got up. Now it is 9 o'clock (A.M.) & all the kiddoes are asleep. Bill says it will take them about a week to get over it!

Bill said there wasn't much to say about "this place," but I have found plenty all ready. On base it is just like being in Florida, but off base - well, it's a different world from anything we're used to seeing - donkey carts, veiled women walking down the road, vegetable stands & little shops on the roadside, with the shopkeeper asleep on a blanket on the ground and it's terribly dusty from the sand. It is all very much as I expected so am not shocked by it as some of the people thought I would. The one thing that did surprise me was the houses, ours included, they are right on the road - you open the gate, go up the steps to the porch and there's the front door! The house itself is quite nice and I think we'll do just fine in it. I can't really describe it except that it is much as Bill said & the floor plan much like he said. The screened porch will probably be the most popular spot in the house. When we get the furniture in we'll take pictures for you.

We are moving in tomorrow so guess we will be rather busy the next few days. I was glad to have the long weekend so Bill would be there to help, but there's going to be a big celebration on the 4th (or for the 4th) so we must take the children to that. There'll be picnics, games, camel rides, & fireworks out over the Med. so to heck with housework - we have 2 1/2 years for that!

The Nusspickles have been so nice the children & I spent Wed. afternoon with her, we went to the club together for dinner and they are keeping the children for us tomorrow & having us for dinner also.

Maj. Swole got 3 rooms for us on base so we'd be close to all the facilities - snack bar, club, PX, etc., but it's a real "dump" so we'll sure be glad to get in the house. This used to be a barracks, I guess, & has a community bath, shower, etc. so isn't too pleasant, but at least we do have beds to sleep in!

The weather isn't bad at all - I have been much hotter at home & the nights are real cool.

So far all is well and I do think we'll enjoy it here.

It sure was good to talk to you the other night before we left. I wish I could have talked longer, but the phone was at the information desk and there were people waiting to use it.

Mother, I can't tell you how much we enjoyed being with you. It was so nice being together, when we will be gone so long. I just hope the confusion wasn't too hard on you and that the house isn't in too bad a shape. We sure do miss you and Billy keeps asking where you are & every time he sees a bus he says "Grandma's Bussy."

I'm out of paper so will write you again as soon as I can. Write us real soon & tell us all about your trip.

We love you. Nance, Bill & kiddoes"

In the thirty years that I worked for the Air Force and Agriculture, the favorite auditor I worked with had to be Frank Nusspickle. He was so exuberant that someone had to hold him back when he was hot on an audit lead. This New Yorker had a quick wit and a fast mouth and was like a little kid with that devilish look in his eyes when he determined that an audit finding existed. He was at his best during audit discussions with Wheelus Commanders and never was at a loss for words or lost a disputed point for lack of fact or opinion.

Frank's Buick was a joke. He would not wash it or put shocks on it, so as he bounced down the Libyan paths called highways, Frank practiced all the bad driving habits he learned in New York City. I tended to choke up when he cut ninety degree corners so close to the Arab shacks. The blast of his exhaust and the Buick's vibration caused noticeable damage to anything around. I've hit the floorboard in his backseat more than once to assure myself that no one noticed that I was a witness to Frank's driving.

Frank's wife, Jo Anne, was from Hasbrouck Heights, New Jersey. Her honeymoon home was the Arab villa in Sukel Juma, Libya. What a way to start a marriage. During those early days of married life Jo Anne experienced many difficulties that other brides could not imagine.

Frank would have gone far in the Air Force if he had decided to make it his career; however, he stayed in Georgia for about one year then resigned his regular commission and returned to New York where he is currently a senior partner in one of the major National CPA firms and has been President of the New York Association of CPAs. Frank later told me that some of his clients were from the middle east. He would not meet these clients there but would meet them in Europe to discuss their accounting and business needs because of the memories he had of those crazy years we spent at Wheelus.

All of the members of the audit staff contributed greatly to the mission of the Auditor General and our local office. Lieutenants Solecki and Fry, Sergeants Wallen and Smith, and Airman Stoutemire, and Mr. Chandler, our only civilian, were assigned at different periods during my two and half years at Wheelus. Each individual had different personalities and abilities, but I have fond memories of each and everyone of them.

Chief Master Sergeant Smith replaced Sgt. Hal Wallen in the summer of 1966 as our NCO auditor. Sgt. Smith was an excellent auditor who produced many outstanding audits during this time. He was extremely conservative and deeply believed in his religious convictions. Due to his beliefs various factions on the base criticized him and made allegations concerning his activities which were never proven. However, Sgt. Smith did hand out Christian literature to Arabs, which was forbidden. When confronted, he discontinued this practice. Due to these circumstances Sgt. Smith's work could have been adversely affected, but was not.

In 1969, Sgt. Smith retired and became a member of the Bob Jones University staff in North Carolina.

The Base officials, including the Wing and Base Commanders, their Deputies, and Staffs (Division and Squadron Commanders) were responsible for managing various operations at the large Wheelus complex consisting of about 3,500 personnel and dependents plus an auxiliary target range located about 100 miles south in the Sahara Desert. The primary mission assigned to Wheelus was to support European command (USAFE) fighter/bomber aircraft and their crews. Every six months these crews flew their jets (F-100's, F-105's and F-4's) in and remained for extended periods of time. While at Wheelus, these crews conducted practice bombing and strafing missions over simulated targets located at the target range. Wheelus maintenance and supply personnel serviced these visiting aircraft and Wheelus support aircraft. The visiting crews were quartered, fed and supported as well.

The base also had secondary missions, including communications and ground radar responsibilities, Military Air Transport Service, regional medical services, and support to the U. S. Embassy operations located in Tripoli. Additionally, other activities were carried out to assure the base was operationally ready in the event of a National Emergency. These included some intelligence operations and maintenance of set quantities of supplies (called Gray Eagle) to be immediately transported to auxiliary airfields in Europe and Africa.

Service operations located on the base included a Post Exchange (PX), Commissary, Housing (Family Quarters, BOQ, NCO/Airman Billets and Visiting Officer/Airman Quarters), Officer, NCO and Airman Clubs, Base Supply, Food Services, and other recreational or morale activities. Professional services included legal, medical, dental, engineering, news media (newspaper and television), and accounting and finance offices.

Colonel Joseph Moody, the Wing Commander, was primarily responsible for all of the above activities. He, therefore delegated authority as much as possible to his subordinate deputies and staff to fulfill the Mission that had been assigned. As Resident Auditor, I worked for the Regional Auditor General, headquartered at Rhine Main AFB, Germany. Thus, our audits were independent of local Command or base influence. If problems between the auditors and base officials could not be satisfactorily resolved locally, they were sent to higher headquarters for resolution. Our audit mission was to audit all the activities noted above periodically and, in some cases, several times each year.

It was imperative therefore, that audit and Base Command have an open and candid relationship. The Wing Commander and his deputies had great responsibilities and their jobs and future careers depended on how effective they were in meeting mission goals and keeping the base operationally ready in event of a National emergency. Our duty as auditors was to make necessary audit examinations to detect problem areas that would affect the base's mission and operational readiness. Our reports should candidly reflect the results of our examinations and be used by base officials to correct the cited deficiencies and thus enhance mission effectiveness and operational readiness. Initially our audit/base relationship was not as good as it should have been. However, when the Wing and Base Commanders and a few of their deputies changed, the relationship greatly improved.

Wheelus underwent two Operational Readiness Inspections (ORI's) by the USAFE Inspector General and his team of about 40 inspectors. The base failed both of these ORI's during the tenure of the first group of commanders. After the Command changed another ORI was performed and the Base successfully passed it.

Colonel Moody, the first Wing Commander (WC), served about fifteen months from the time I arrived at Wheelus. During the summer of 1966 Colonel Joseph White assumed the command. From the viewpoint of most observers, Colonel Moody was more concerned with his political affiliations with Libyan and U.S. Embassy officials than with the primary mission of operating the auxiliary target range and supporting the visiting USAFE crews and their aircraft. Since Moody spent so much of his time with the secondary political responsibilities he delegated much of his authority to subordinate officers to manage Wing/Base operations. As a result, many activities were not adequately managed. Needed coordination between various elements of command were lacking and control over resources (personnel, material, and money) was far from adequate. Since Command did not have adequate control, ineffective management resulted and most of the effort at all levels consisted of "putting out fires" rather than conducting normally effective operations. It was easy to understand why the Base was not ready when an unannounced ORI occurred.

During Colonel Moody's tenure I was invited into his office once. He established a procedure that all audits would be discussed with his Vice Wing Commander (VWC) who transferred to Wheelus in the late summer of 1965, about the time I assumed the Resident Auditor duties from Tom Swole.

Since the WC was most concerned with his political relationships, he delegated management authority and responsibility to Colonel John Patton, the VWC, and the Base Commander. Without strong leadership at the top, various elements of management and operations eroded seriously.

Colonel Patton relied heavily on his subordinates, and in many cases they failed him. Problems noted in ORI reviews and our audits were mainly caused by inadequate control at middle management levels. Patton did not have the ability to instill sufficient pride in his staff to manage the operations effectively. As a result, any outside review group or inspection team could quickly detect soft spots in supposedly controlled operations and defective management practices.

When we discussed these problem areas with the Colonel Patton, he would become extremely defensive, would often side with his staff members who had let him down, and would not take adequate corrective actions to solve known problems. Thus management control deteriorated and base operations did not meet Mission objectives.

During the spring of 1966, a surprise ORI was performed, management practices were evaluated and found wanting. As a result, the Wing and Base commanders were transferred Stateside. The VWC remained at Wheelus. Shortly, Colonel Joe White transferred in as the new WC. Within two months, Col. White decided that he wanted a new VWC, so Colonel Patton transferred to another base in England. Col. Bill Evans, who had been the Chief of Operations at Wheelus took over as VWC.

I had a short chat with Colonel Patton at his going away dinner and he confided that he had not been tough enough, he had listened to the wrong people, and should have heeded the warnings that we reported to him in our audits. Thus, he should have gained a great deal of experience during his tour at Wheelus.

Col. Sheldon West had been the Base Commander at Wheelus for about two years when I arrived. He was in charge of all base activities and had minimal help from his superiors. Col. West was always on the run putting out fires caused by irresponsible subordinates. Many thought, as I did, that Col. West would not delegate authority, but tried to be on the spot to do everything himself. However, it didn't take me long to find out that if West was not around to see the job completed, it would not be done. Thus, he was on call twenty-four hours each day and many times he was on the scene of an event that had occurred at three or four A.M.

I had no problems discussing audit results with Col. West. He was receptive to recommendations that would improve operations, and when problem areas surfaced where he needed audit advice, he would contact me for an audit opinion. During some audit discussions where our audits clearly reported stupid actions on the part of Base personnel, it was easy to see the anger in Col. West's eyes. One day he was tossing a softball in the air while he listened to our report. At one point when the discussion got heated with the officer in charge, I thought "look out" he's going to throw the ball at the head of the officer who was responsible for the audit condition. If he had, I would not have blamed him. However, Col. West was a gentleman and always managed to control his temper. His next assignment was at McGuire AFB, New Jersey. and when families arrived at McGuire after being evacuated from Wheelus during the six day war, the first person they saw as they deplaned was Col. West welcoming them back home and offering them needed assistance.

Col. Joe White arrived at Wheelus with a broom and a plan. He immediately formed details of troops to clean up the base on a daily basis. He brought in a new Base Commander, fired the VWC, and reassigned Col. Evans to the VWC position. Col. White was highly visible on the base and to many onlookers' surprise, gave up much of the relationship with the U. S. Embassy. According to White, Wheelus was an Air Force Base first and foremost. Political activity all but ceased. Maybe Tom Swole's report that got him transferred had some impact after all.

Joe White opened his door to me and supported our audit efforts whole heartedly. Early in his tour, I gained his confidence when I briefed him on a serious maintenance problem that concerned aircraft safety. A F-100 had flown 20 hours after it should have been grounded for a required time compliance tech order part change. Col. White told me that a similar condition occurred at a previous base. A crewman of a B-47 was lost through a hatch door that required maintenance that had been overlooked.

Col. White had a great sense of humor and because of his insistence on a clean, well kept base he was dubbed Mr. Clean. Adamant airmen who were not accustomed to serving on cleanup details, every so often slipped up to White's quarters during the night and painted graffiti on his mailbox. He would have his mailbox repainted only to have it messed up again. This went on for some time, until the art work ceased. Joe White said that he missed these occurrences and may be getting too soft.

Joe White believed in being fit. He played tennis with the younger officers and ran two or more miles every day. He was interested in the sports programs and helped me coach one of the four football teams we had for the troops and family recreation. He lasted only three weeks as my assistant coach because some of his staff members felt he was showing favoritism to one group of athletes.

Joe White's new VWC was the respected young colonel, Bill Evans who had run a "tight ship" as Operations Director for the prior Command. Thus, when Col. White selected Evans as his VWC, no one was surprised to see how well Evans worked with White and managed his new duties. Col. Evans called on our staff to perform special audits and he was an officer who welcomed audit recommendations that improved base operational capabilities.

In 1970, when I left the Air Force I asked Col. Evans for a job reference. He sent me the following letter that I'll always treasure. This reference helped me greatly in securing an auditor position with the USDA Office of Inspector General.

> TO WHOM IT MAY CONCERN:
> SUBJECT: Letter of Evaluation
>
> 1. From August 1964 until May 1967, I was stationed at Wheelus Air Base, Tripoli, Libya, filling the positions of Deputy Commander for Operations and Vice Commander, 7272 Flying Training Wing. In those capacities, I had numerous occasions to deal with the resident auditor. Major (then Captain) William L. Lively was assigned to that position during my tour.
>
> 2. Auditors, due to the nature of their job, normally do not enjoy the best rapport with base personnel. This situation is usually aggravated by the auditors themselves, who are often prone to flaunt their authority in the face of senior commanders. It did not take me long to realize that Captain Lively was not a typical auditor. Obviously well schooled technically for the difficult and complex projects which his office was assigned, he

additionally had the personality and attitude which bred cooperation and harmony with the base and wing personnel. His approach of helpfulness, rather than cold investigations and criticism, was refreshing to find. As a result, the commanders on the base actively solicited Captain Lively's counsel and assistance in solving many of the base problems. His mature judgment on command matters of concern heavily influenced the courses of action that were taken. He voluntarily assisted staff and command sections alike in working out management tools and administrative procedures in order to insure proper controls.

3. Without hesitation, I can unequivocally identify Captain Lively as a person who has unquestioned integrity, a large capacity for work, and a wealth of knowledge and experience in the field of auditing. He constantly seeks additional responsibilities and will subvert personal desires in order to accomplish his assignments. He will be a valuable asset to any organization.

s./ William J Evans
WILLIAM J. EVANS
Brigadier General, USAF
Deputy Director for Concepts and
Operational Readiness

Col. Evans served two successful tours of duty as a combat Wing Commander in Viet Nam where he was highly acclaimed and decorated. He retired from service in 1978 as a four star general.

Col. George Dorman succeeded Col. West as the Base Commander in 1966. His credentials were impressive as he had been General Curtis LeMay's aide for several years and served most of his career in the Strategic Air Command (SAC), as had Col. Joe White.

When Joe White furnished the broom, George Dorman furnished most of the manpower to use it. Several new officers arrived at Wheelus during the summer of 1966 and slowly but surely the base posture began taking shape. Preventive measures to offset ongoing problems were initiated in sensitive areas. Instead of putting out fires, George Dorman instituted improvements to management systems. His staff, including Lt. Col. Neal Meurlin the new Comptroller, followed his lead and base operations shifted into high gear and was off to the races.

We continued to issue audit reports showing the areas where improvements were needed. Col. Dorman and his staff generally accepted our reports, but they would argue if "gray areas" were reported and different opinions prevailed. We won some and lost some, but resolved the disputes locally and both the base and our audit staff profited from these occurrences.

In 1967, I was promoted to Major. Lt Col. Meurlin brought a pair of his old oak leaves and attached them to my collar. That afternoon, I came home and found a dirty pair of old sneakers on the living room floor with oak leaves pinned on the toe of each shoe, compliments of Jim Baker. At least I got promoted the first time I was eligible.

Early in 1967, the new command of White, Evans, and Dorman faced their first unannounced ORI. The Air Force Inspectors from Europe were at Wheelus for over a week. They held their exit briefing at the Base Theater, where all officials gathered to hear the outcome. Wheelus had passed its ORI! The first time in three years.

After the exit briefing, I immediately walked the four blocks back to my office and found Col. Dorman sitting in the chair behind my desk. The Colonel said that our audits were one of the major reasons for Wheelus passing the ORI, and he thanked me for our past efforts. I was stunned that George Dorman would have such high regard for the audit staff's endeavors. Since we were an agency that usually received little credit for the work we undertook, this was one time in my life that I was at a loss for words.

In June 1967, The Israeli-Egyptian Six Day War occurred and Egyptian President Nasser broadcast that American jets from Wheelus had flown high cover for the Israelis over Egypt. Riots broke out in Tripoli and any non Arabic individual was in peril. Col. Dorman took the lead in organizing manpower to shift the base mission to a war-time setting. Over

6,000 civilians and military dependents were housed at Wheelus in all available quarters and were evacuated to the States or Europe by air within a week. This major undertaking was handled in an outstanding manner. Much of the credit for this distinguished effort belonged to Col. Dorman.

In 1969, Col. Dorman lost his life in an aircraft mishap over Vietnam. The Air force lost an outstanding officer who had great ability to fulfill any mission assigned.

Over the years, when I think of my two and a half year tour at Wheelus, I often feel it was the worst experience in my life. Yet, many of the experiences I had there are clearly etched in my mind 30+ years later. The characteristics of the audit staff and the Wing/Base Command would make any Resident Auditor's life interesting. Mine was far from dull.

Most auditors would have been overwhelmed at the number and significance of the audit findings that occurred at Wheelus. It appeared that NCOs, airmen, and others with little to do in their leisure time would scheme and devise methods to help themselves to available Government funds and property.

NCO and Officer Club (open Messes) were prime targets for fraudulent schemes. Government lumber, building supplies, and other material were diverted to personal use. Liquor and other items were black-marketed to non Air Force personnel. Above all, management decisions were often questionable and internal control over sensitive assets was almost nonexistent. These factors and the trend for persons to neglect their duties were the things my staff and I faced upon my arrival. They were the issues that set off the bomb called Wheelus.

Several of our audits reported conditions so serious that they were elevated to Air Force level in Washington. Many actions reported concerning Wheelus personnel and management were so unbelievable that they were humorous. I am amazed that the turnabout caused by new commanders was so dramatic. I shudder to think how the base would have reacted to the Six Day War if had occurred in early 1965 rather than 1967.

NCO and Offiers' Clubs paid no rent. The club's primary expenses were payroll costs, furniture and equipment, band and entertainer fees, and food and liquor costs. Liquor was purchased from the Base Class Six Store at about $1.50 per quart and food from the base commissary at wholesale costs. Personnel costs in 1965 was about $1.50 per hour. Thus, proceeds from $7.00 per month dues from about 500 members and substantial markups for dining room and bar sales should have allowed the NCO Club to reap large profits. However, this was not the case as little or no profits were experienced. Moreover, Club members did not receive many free meals or other returns from the Club.

The NCO Club was the gathering place for most NCO's and their families after work and on weekends. The Club had a huge foyer where about 30 slot machines lined it's walls. The play on these machines was continuous and the Club should have gained high profits from them.

Since the Club showed little or no profit each month, why did this happen? That was the question to be answered during an audit that Lt. Frank Nusspickle and Sgt. Hal Wallen made in the fall of 1965.

We did not know how deep the water was when we first waded into the audit, but Frank and Hal quickly learned that to keep afloat they would probably need a lifejacket because the waters were dark, deep, and wide. Some Club custodians (managers) were a breed of individuals who were highly suspect. The most successful would connive, deal, or break established rules to accomplish their objectives. Others took advantage of loose internal control over cash, food or liquor inventories or other management practices to rip-off Club resources. The chief master sergeant who was the custodian was a master of all the above noted traits. He had devised several schemes to pocket as much money as he could.

Since the average bottle of liquor cost the Club about $1.50 per quart and considering a ten percent loss due to spillage and an occasional free drink, a bartender could pour about 28 one ounce drinks per quart bottle. The Club charged the customer 50 cents per drink; thus, the bar should have realized cash receipts of about $14.00 and earned a gross profit of about

$12..50 per bottle. On an average day three to four hundred customers would consume about 20 bottles and gross profits should have totaled about $250 per day or about $7,500 per month for liquor sales alone. This would not include beer sale profits. Monthly profit and loss statements did not show these profits from bar sales.

Frank and Hal reviewed the bar's inventory records and quickly found that ending daily inventories taken at the close of business did not agree with the inventories taken at the beginning of the next day's operations. In some cases, it looked like several cases of booze walked out of the door between the time consecutive inventories were taken. To compound the problem Frank checked out the bar's shot glasses used to pour drinks. To his amazement when he poured 32 shots of water into a quart container the container was only 3/4's full. Thus, Frank deduced that Management had replaced the standard one ounce shot glasses with 3/4 ounce ones. Bar patrons were therefore being poured short drinks and Management had more available booze to steal.

At this point, I immediately contacted Mr. Bob Brooding, Executive Officer, Base Office of Special Investigation (OSI), to request assistance in investigating Club management. He assigned an agent to assist Frank and Hal. The combined audit/investigation determined that large losses of liquor had taken place. Since there were two to three thousand oil company workers residing in or about Tripoli who could not purchase liquor at $1.50 per quart but were forced to pay high taxed prices on the Libyan economy, the custodian had a ready market for the stolen liquor. He probably netted about $30, 000 to $40,000 per year on this black market operation.

After the audit/investigation was completed, Command decided to fire the custodian, give him an Article 15 admonishment, which is less severe than a General Court Marshal, and demand his retirement from the Air Force. All of his retirement benefits remained in tact. After retirement, he immediately settled in Europe and began selling slot machines throughout the European theater of military operations (Europe, Africa, and the Middle East).

About two months after the custodian had retired, his replacement confided to Colonel West that a potential new condition had arisen. Colonel West contacted me and asked that I meet with him and the new custodian to discuss what was wrong. When I arrived, Colonel West stated that the new custodian had been given $1,800 in cash by the agent who furnished the Club bands and entertainers. The agent operated an entertainment agency in Germany and furnished various bands and entertainers to American Military Officer and NCO Clubs located in the European theater.

According to the entertainment agent, the reason for the rebate was that the band he furnished in the prior month was not worth the $18,000 he received for their services. He further suggested to the new custodian that this rebate was not unusual. When the custodian dropped the agent off at the Tripoli airport, the agent left the $1,800 on the front seat of the custodian's car. Since the new custodian knew that we may still be investigating Club management he decided to take the money to the Base Commander.   Colonel West asked me how the Club should handle this transaction. I replied that this was obviously a kickback from the agent who had been paid about $200,000 annually by the Wheelus NCO Club. If the agent had kicked back ten percent of previous proceeds to the departed prior custodian, he would have received about $20,000 within the prior year from this scam. To my knowledge the prior custodian was never confronted with this possible fraudulent action and the entertainment agent continued to furnish the Club with entertainers and bands.

Since this entertainment agency furnished entertainers and bands throughout the area, I contacted the Regional Audit Headquarters in Germany and suggested that they should have their auditors obtain the agent's accounting records to determine if he was recording rebates to the Wheelus club and other clubs for tax credit purposes. If so, the accounting entries could be traced back to various club records to determine if kickbacks were occurring elsewhere. Early in 1966, an auditor and an OSI agent visited the agent and requested his accounting records. Under the terms of standard contract provisions used by Club activities, contractor records were to be made available for such audit purposes. The entertainment agent told his Air Force visitors that they could not examine his records and if they did so, he would sue the U.S. Government. To my knowledge his records were never examined.

In 1970, entertainment agents, high ranking military officers and enlisted personnel in Europe and Asia were indicted for similar kickback activities. These events were reported for weeks on TV and other media. Many officials testified before a Senate Committee, and several members of the armed forces were sentenced to prison terms and removed from the Services. It certainly took a long time for the nation to find out what we determined four years earlier at Wheelus.

Wheelus operated a small communication site detachment approximately one hundred miles due east of Wheelus on the main road to Bengasi. The site used radio, radar, and other navigational communication equipment to monitor and control incoming/outgoing aviation traffic. It was manned by a detachment of nine airmen.

During our NCO Club audit we noted that much liquor had been sent to the site to stock a bar in the Club annex located there. Since we found many problems at the Wheelus Club, I decided to send Lt. Jerry Solecki and Sgt. Wallen to the site to perform a small audit and determine if operations were properly managed.

Jerry and Hal spent a couple of days at the site, came back to the office and wrote their report. They reviewed records for a twelve month period and found that the airmen and possibly others had misused liquor supplies and gasoline inventories.

Jerry and Hal found that each of the nine airmen assigned to the site would have had to drink six quarts of liquor each day for the past year to use amounts that had been issued to the NCO annex. When Jerry and Hal computed the annual gasoline consumption, they determined that the airmen would have had to driven the 1 1/2 ton truck assigned to the site twenty four hours per day, at 50 miles per hour, at a four miles per gallon usage rate, for the entire 365 days of the past year to consume the gasoline issued to the detachment.

Since it was apparent that the airmen and others were committing fraud, we referred the case to OSI who conducted a limited investigation. They concluded that the site airmen, in collusion with our old "friend"" the prior NCO Club custodian had been selling liquor and gasoline to oil company employees. This black-market operation was quite profitable to those involved.

Black-marketing was illegal under U.S. Military law but also violated Libyan laws concerning taxation on imported liquor, gasoline and other items. The base recalled the airmen and conducted successful court marshal actions on each of them. However, the prior custodian never faced these charges since he had previously retired from the service.

We earlier stated that the Officer and NCO Clubs generated a great amount of revenue from the members' play of slot machines. The Clubs had machines in their main locations, annexes, and snack bars. Around the base there were six or seven locations where a person with extra change burning a hole in his pocket could feed it to a waiting slot.

With so many machines available Club employees and others would devise schemes to pilfer the slot's coins. During the 2 1/2 years that I was at Wheelus, we noted five or six different methods individuals would use to steal from the slots. Supposedly, management devised procedures to control cash after it was removed from them. However, clever individuals knew that they could override these controls. Many did.

Some of the ways crooked employees used to steal the money from slot machines follow. Mechanics with a second set of slot keys could empty tubes of coins in the slots when they worked on them. When employees counted the coins after a day's operations they could record a lower number than counted and pocket the difference. Other employees would forge payout records to obtain cash.

In most instances these schemes proved successful until someone "squealed" on the culprit or an audit or investigation luckily detected them. However, I'm sure there were many other ways successful thieves used to carry out their cunning schemes.

One Monday morning Bob Brooding called and asked if we would help them because the Skin-divers Club had been broken into late the preceding night. One of their two slot machines had been cracked open and its contents had been stolen. Other items may have also been taken.

The Custodian told us that besides the loss of about $200 from the slot machine other merchandise was missing. He had taken an inventory and claimed that about 50 cases of beer and 25 cases of soft drinks were gone. He felt that someone had come in by boat late at night, broken into the Club, cracked open one of the two slots and taken the beer and soda.

Neither we nor the OSI ever proved who robbed the Club, but we both felt that the beer and soft drinks were not taken during the break-in. Inventory shortages were probably occurring regularly and possibly the Custodian felt that because of the break-in he could balance his books and make up the shortages by claiming the missing stocks were stolen. Whoever broke into the Club would have had an easier time cracking open the second slot machine for an additional $200, than lugging 75 cases of beers and soda down the sandy Mediterrain beach to a waiting boat.

We decided to look at the warehousing of supplies so I sent Lt. Jerry Solecki to Base Supply to survey what we needed to review. After a day or so, Jerry dropped by the office and related that a major warehouse was being used to store an excessive amount of toilet paper. Based on this astonishing news I told Jerry to dig into this revelation, give me hard facts and figures fast, and get down to the bottom line results.

Two hours later, Jerry returned and stated that the largest warehouse on base was crammed full of the hygienic need. The toilet paper had been left there when the Air Force Area Depot departed Wheelus over 10 years ago and no toilet paper was being shipped elsewhere since they left. We immediately sat down at our calculators and began compiling statistics.

Based on the Military population at Wheelus, about 1,500 airmen, we came up with the following figures.

Cases of toilet paper on hand	25,000
(X) Rolls per Case	120
Rolls on Hand	3,000,000
# of Airmen	1,500
Rolls for each Airman	2,000
Sheets per Roll	300
Sheet per each Airman	600,000
Liberal usage per day	50(2)
Days to used daily amount of toilet paper	12,000
Days per year	365
Years to use the toilet paper	32.9

(1) Only Base military personnel use the paper. Dependents had to purchase their own toilet paper at the Commissary

(2) Computed on two sittings per day. Twenty five sheets per sitting.

If we had included a 50% contingency factor for excess usage of 75 sheets per day per Airman caused by the infamous Tripoli Trots (dysentery), it would have taken 21.9 years to consume all the paper.

When I discussed this significant occurrence with the Director of Material, I asked if he would like my formal report to be written on a roll of the subject paper or would the regular report format be acceptable. The Colonel laughed and replied that the normal format would be more than sufficient. Whenever the base was to be closed, I suggested that we should leave the paper with the Libyans. However, due to their customs and questionable hygienic standards, they would probably not know what the paper was for and would try to use it for stationery.

During the 1960s a major undertaking by each Air Force activity was to cut costs and document the results of efforts in cost reduction reports. Since the Resident Auditor was an independent agency on the base, we had to review and validate each cost reduction report and certify that the action taken met the requirements set forth in cost reduction guidelines. Bases were rated on their submissions of cost reductions to the Major Air

Commands and in some cases military officers were judged on meeting cost reduction goals.

Once the Civil Engineering section submitted a cost reduction item to us for our review and evaluation that looked pretty good. Their narrative stated that the Base had been sending electrical motors to Malta weekly for repairs. Since last year, the motors were sent on the weekly flight to Malta. The weekly flights were made to send news stories to Maltese printers for inclusion in the weekly Tripoli Trotter base news paper published there.

The cost reduction action had been well prepared and reported that about $60,000 of annual costs had been saved over the past year. The action stated that workmanship in Malta was much better than in a downtown Tripoli repair facility and the costs were also much lower. Cost comparisons between the Maltese and Tripoli repair facilities were shown. The action also stated that a specific civil service employee assigned to the Civil Engineering section had previously submitted this action to the Base Suggestion Award Committee where it had been approved. The civilian employee received a $300 cash award. A Tripoli Trotter clipping was attached which included a picture of Wing Commander Moody presenting the $300 check and congratulating the employee for his suggestion.

I told Frank Nusspickle that this cost reduction action should be easy to validate and approve. It should not take him more than 15 minutes to go over to Procurement and substantiate the facts with the sergeant who was in charge of small procurement. Four hours later, Frank returned and laid the following on me. The sergeant in procurement was madder than hell about this action. The employee had pushed this suggestion through last year and Procurement sent three motors to Malta immediately after the suggestion was approved. It took the Maltese repair shop twice as long to do the same job, the workmanship was terrible, and to top it off, the Maltese costs were much higher. Thus, Procurement had not sent any more motors to Malta in the past year.

Frank surmised that the Civil Engineer employee must have estimated how many motors had been sent to Malta during the past year, guessed at the costs, and used these figures to record the savings when he submitted the cost reduction action to us. I told Frank that we would disapprove the cost reduction, and since it appeared that the whole thing stunk, let's write an audit report and make certain recommendations.

Frank went to work and the next day he and I met with VWC Colonel Patton and a Lt. Colonel who was the Civil Engineer. We briefed these two officers on the findings and asked the Civil Engineer why he approved the original suggestion concerning motors sent to Malta? How did they come up with the monetary savings, and foremost, why did the Civil Engineer employee receive a $300 cash award for a false suggestion? The Civil Engineer did not have responsive answers to these questions.

We told Colonel Patton that our recommendations would be: (1) Assure suggestions and cost reduction actions are factual before submission for approval; (2) Assure reviewing/approving officers make actual reviews to substantiate facts before approval; and (3) Have the Civil Engineer employee return the $300 he received. At that point, Colonel Patton started "chewing" on the Civil Engineer so Frank and I excused ourselves and left. On the way out of the front door Frank chided me and said that I left out the most important recommendation. When I asked what? He replied that I should have recommended that the "Trotter" publish another article and include a picture of the employee returning the $300 to Colonel Moody. In my 30 years of Government Service this was the only time I saw a monetary award returned by the recipient.

One Sunday afternoon about one P.M., Frank dropped by our villa in glorious Sukel Juma. He laughed and said that a sergeant came up to him after the morning Mass and was very upset. He told Frank that the new computer hardware was being installed at the main Base Supply warehouse and the "Brass" decided that an office for terminal operators should be built beside the computer room. Thus, he and about ten other NCOs and airmen had spent two weeks working on this office space. Early this Sunday morning, Colonels Moody, Patton, and West and other officers visited the computer complex. They looked over the work on the new office beside the computer room which was about 90% complete. At that point they ordered the supply personnel to tear the office down.

The sergeant complained that he and the others had wasted a lot of time and materials in doing this work, when they should have been inventorying $6 million of supplies on hand to assure that accurate inventory records would be loaded into the new computer's data file. Frank agreed with the sergeant that someone had screwed up royally. I told Frank to cool it for today, but tomorrow go to supply and find out what was going on.

About 10 A.M. on Monday, Frank came bounding into the office and said his buddy, the sergeant, and other supply personnel were down on their knees using blow torches to burn off vinyl tile that had been glued to 1800 square feet of concrete floor in the warehouse. They had already knocked down the office walls, plywood paneling and 2X4 studding. Other used building material was stacked in several piles nearby.

Frank said that most of the materials had been filched from the Gray Eagle package stocks, which were to be used only during the outbreak of war or other national emergency. He also found out that no one had obtained the required approval from Hq. USAFE to build the office complex. That was the reason that the Wing Commander and his staff halted construction work and ordered the completed work to be dismantled.

Frank and I agreed that we needed to see the VWC about this situation. So, that afternoon we interviewed Colonel Patton and told him that we would have to contact our Auditor General Regional Office to determine what course of action they wanted us to take. Report the condition, or not.

Colonel Patton gave us his version of the story and Frank recorded it. Patton felt that some of the troops got a little too exuberant and started construction without the required approval; however, not much had occurred. Patton asked that I give him a copy of my letter to the Regional Office. I agreed.

Frank and I wrote the letter which included Colonel Patton's comments, the facts as we saw them, and a cost estimate of time and materials used.

We mailed the letter, and later after the mail had departed Wheelus, I hand carried the copy over to Colonel Patton. He read the letter and blew a fuse. He accused me of misquoting him, said that he would have the matter investigated, and demanded that I not send the letter to my Regional Office. I told him that the letter had already been mailed. He insisted that I write a retraction. After much heated discussion, I told Patton that I would not write a retraction but suggested that he write the Regional Auditor General and tell his side of the story. Patton agreed to this and would furnish me a copy of his letter. Colonel Patton toned down his letter to my bosses and inferred that he, Frank, and I had a communication break down when we discussed the condition. He also stated in his letter that he had set up an investigation to determine why this condition occurred.

Later, the Regional Office instructed me not to report the matter since the base was conducting its own investigation. A Legal Office major conducted the investigation which took about three months. His written report and attachments were about 2 inches thick. It reported that several hundred dollars worth of materials were misused and Gray Eagle stocks were improperly tampered with. The investigation recommended that 3 officers responsible should be given at least letters of reprimand. To my knowledge his recommendations were never carried out.

It is my opinion that because of over reactions, much of the above was unnecessary. In effect, because someone broke a rule, Command made a questionable decision to tear down an office that was 90% complete and was probably needed, sensitive Government material was wasted, supply man hours were wasted, the investigator's and other personnel's time were wasted, and, overall nothing resulted from the extended exercise. Such escapades were common at Wheelus.

We later performed an audit of the Gray Eagle activity and found that of four packages of materials (lumber, tools, housekeeping/food service equipment, and other materials needed to maintain an operating base) only one was complete. The other three were from 35 to 60% operational. I hate to think what would have happened if a real national emergency had occurred.

The only thing that kept our morale up was the friends and some of the activities available at Wheelus. The friends you made remained the closest you would have in your entire life. Thirty plus years after Wheelus these people remain soundly etched in my thoughts, and I try to keep in touch with most, if I can. Peg and Stark Sanders, Frank and Jo Anne Nusspickle, Neil and Phyllis Meurlin, Bob and Joan Brooding, Pat and Kathy Jones, and my auditors and staff and many others made Wheelus life bearable.

When I arrived at Wheelus, Captain Stark Sanders, a legal officer, took me to his villa to see what the living quarters would be like. I made a mistake of leaving the front door open as I left, so Peg Sanders shouted "were you brought up in a barn?." Since flies were in abundance in Libya, I felt she had a good point. From that point on, I have had a great relationship with Peg and both Nancy and I have loved her like a sister.

Every Sunday morning after church, couples would go to the Officers Club for lunch. We would all set around a long table and give our orders to the Libyan waiter. Since more and more people showed up, the waiter got upset, threw down his tray and walked out. I'm not sure if he ever came back.

My children liked living in Libya, Jan took an educational trip on an English ship that carried students to Bengasi, Libya, Egypt, Lebanon, Cyprus, and Greece. She was gone for two weeks, and will always remember that experience.

Mike was involved in the Scouts and Little League baseball. He was a pretty good pitcher and a better catcher. Both Mike and Len, were water boys for the football team I coached. The first year, my team the Bulldogs lost all nine games we played. The second year, we got a few better players and won four and lost five. The third year, we were leading the four man league when I transferred back to the States. Regardless of whether we won or lost, we had a post game party in back of our villa.

Billy was only two when he arrived at Wheelus, but he became great friends with James Baker, the son of Jim and Tina Baker. During the Six Day War, when Nancy and the kids were evacuated to Spain and later the U.S. Billy spotted James at the airport in Spain and both ran up to each other and hugged and cried out James, James and Billy, Billy. Billy sucked his thumb, but when our neighbor, Joe Fernandez, who Billy adored, got on him, he immediately stopped the thumb sucking. One day, in the side yard Billy told his mother to come out and see the big black bug. It turned out to be a scorpion. They were abundant in the area.

We had a well that supplied wash water. Drinking water was carried in from the base. To keep the algae out of the tank on top of our roof, I did what a lot of folks did, put in gold fish to dispose of the algae. However I didn't put a screen over the tank's outlet to the faucets below in the house. As a result, the fish got caught in the pipes and we had pieces of fish, guts and scales floating in our bathtub.

In February 1967, our 12 year old Jan boarded an English ship for an educational voyage around the Mediterranean for two weeks. She kept the following journal of her trip.

"Jan Lively

1st Day   Mon.

On my first day I woke up at 7:00 and we left for the front gate to wait for the buses to come. When they finally came I kissed everyone good-by and the bus drove to the dock. We went through customs & then we got our suitcases and climbed up the steps of the gangway. It was scary with a heavy suitcase in hand and things on my shoulder. The steps were wet & wobbly! We went straight to our dormitorys after climbing down several flights of stairs.

The rest of the day we just loafed around on deck. After we had left the harbor it started getting rough and all of the kids went around with their heads in brown bags! I was sick but I didn't throw up like every one else did!

2nd Day   Tue

Last night was very restless in that bunk! Today every one was still sick. We went to an assembly. We learned what we would be doing on the ship.

In the afternoon we arrived in Benghazi. There was a band out to meet us! We didn't get off but some British kids got on. They were very nice. Almost everyone from Tripoli is over their seasickness, but the kids from Benghazi didn't feel well.

3rd Day   Wed

We spent all day on board the ship. It was a regular school day. There are 6 periods 3 in mor & 3 in noon. We had Deck Games & Swimming, Reading and Recreation, classrooms.The meals are O.K. except they have potatoes every meal!

I went to the movies with my friend.

4th Day   Thur.

Today we went to Crete. In the morning we went to some ruins in Heraklion. They were the ruins of Knosos. It was an old civilization like the Greeks. The ruins were rebuilt very well. They were rebuilt by an English man. There was a thrown room. the queens room, the sacrificial room, the storage rooms, bedrooms & beautiful staircase. There were the crazy kinds of cloumns. Oh I can't draw them but I hope my pictures come out well.

We also went to the Heraklion Museum where we saw lots of old jewelry and pots and vases and old wall decorations pieced together. We also saw two old skeletons of some of the ancient people. One Male, One Female. They were very interesting.

We went shopping in the afternoon. There were the nicest little shops. I bought a ring, a carving knife for Mike, a shell animal for Billy, and embrodried bag, a flag of Knosos, some postcards (which I lost) and two necklaces, all for $3.50!

5th Day   Fri.

We spent a regular class day on the boat. Some of my friends went swimming, but I thought it was to cold. I went to the movies it was called Ali Babas Sword.

I have made friends with some of the master of arms. They are real nice. I know 2 of their names, Mr. Short and Mr. Hugh ? I also met two others.

We got a good meal today for a change- fish and chips!

6th Day   Sat.

Today we got to Alexandria in Egypt. We had to wake up early to get off of the ship. As we were getting off of the ship I noticed that the customs building was very modern. Out on the street were tour buses ready to take us to Cairo. It would be a 4 hour drive. Our group of girls were in a bus where some boys in the 7th grade from our school and some High School boys. After two hours of driving we stopped at a rest house where we got some cokes. A boy in 7th grade bought us some rock candy. We girls enjoyed it. I hang around with 2 6th grade girls and 2 girls my age.

When we got to Cairo I could see the pyramids in the back ground. They were very pretty from there. First of all we went to the Egyptian Museum. We saw lots of old things taken from the pyramids and the Pharohs tombs. I saw wrapped up mummys, caskets, shrines, face masks, and all sorts of things. Some of the things are made with pure gold! You should have seen the way those things were guarded! I saw a mummified baby, it was all black and skinny. It was out of its wrappings. We wanted to go down to the mummy room but the guide said it cost 2$! I really did

After that we went to the large Mosque where Mohammed Ali is buried. It is so beautiful there. We all had to wear these sort of slippers on top of our shoes to show our respect. On the inside it was beautiful. It had beautiful carpets. And chandelers, millions of them, lit up place. on the outside was a beautiful view of Cairo. I bought some braclets and some postcards. I don't know what happened to all my postcards. After leaving the Mosque we went to an outdoor resturant and ate our packed lunches. There was a beautiful view of the Nile and Cairo.

Then we went to the buses. We left heading toward the pyramids. They were built on a kind of desert plateau.. A girl friend & I started up the inside of the pyramid. It was awful. The steps were simply bars of mettle on a sloping concrete walk. There were 300 of these so called steps. And do you know what we saw when we finally got to the top? A big black suffocating room.

After that we went to the Sphinx. We saw a temple of granite, too. I hope I can go there again sometime.

Then we started back to Alexandrea. We to the desert road back to the ship. It was 10:00 by the time we got back!

7th Day   Sun.

I went to church with some of my friends. It seemed odd to sit in a rocking church. It was a British type service and the first hymn we sang was God save the Queen!

The rest of the day we did whatever we wanted. I sat in a deck-chair almost all afternoon. I did some home work. I went to a movie, but it was so awful I walked down to the dormitory in 1/2 hour after it started. I took a shower and got ready for bed. Good Night

8th Day   Mon.

Today we arrived in Beirut. In the morning we went shopping. Our group went to the gold suik. That's where you get all the nice jewelry. I bought a small crusaders cross necklace, a koran necklace, a gold ring for Len, a charm, and a plaque. We went to this kind of grocery store and asked for a Lebanese sandwich, so the guy cuts a kind of bread for each person. He put some creamy like filling in it. Not until we bought them and taken a bite did we realize the filling was sour cream!

In the afternoon we went on a tour of Byblos. On the way we saw many missionaries at the tops of the mountains. We saw the cable cars going up the side of the mountain to reach the statue of the lady of Lebanon. It was very picturesque.

We were kind of disappointed when we got to Byblos because there really wasn't much there. There was a crusaders castle and 6 Roman columns (the tallest ones left that were built by the Romans). Oh yes, there was a theater too. It was all built close to the sea. Then we went back to the ship. It was a beautiful drive back. I didn't go anywhere tonight but I washed my hair and took a shower. I went to supper at 9:00 and had cocoa. Supper on the ship is a bedtime snack. Good night

9th Day   Tue

We had a regular class day. I went swimming and boy was it cold. Do you know that they put salt water in the pool? It was awful! We just stayed in for 20 min. Two other girls and I played table tennis, then we watched some kids playing deck hockey.

Oh yes the other day (I forgot when) we went up to the bridge let me tell you, was it ever windy. We saw all of the instruments and everything. The wind almost blew us back down the stairs!

I went to a spy movie it was O. K. Then I went to supper then my bunk. Good-night

10th Day   Wed.

Today we arrived in Greece. In the morning we could go wherever we wanted to. We were docked in the port of Piareus. It was about 15 - 20 miles away from Athens. After walking through Piareus for a few minutes our group caught a subway for Athens. It was a twenty minute ride through several other stations till we got there. We got off in the square at Athens.

We went all over the place. I got lost twice but they found me! We bought several goodies in the bakeries. We thought they were wonderful because you can't get that kind of pastry at Wheelus. I bought a ballet picture & perfume, and a lighter for Dad. Then we went back to the train station. We got there just in time. I went into a car where I thought the other girls were, but as it ended up I found out I was in it all alone. I was so scared. Those Greek people probably thought I was crazy because I kept asking where we were. Finally I could regonize the right station by the collered glass ceiling! As I got off the train I found that the other girls were in the same train, and one girl was in the same situation as me! On our way back to the boat we stopped at a little shop and I bought a greek hat for Mike, two little plates of the parthenon, and a salt bust of a Greek god (I think). When we got back to the boat, as I started to get on, my two little plates dropped and broke. I dug around in my purse and found 10 Dracnis (sp?). With that I bought a large plate of the Parthenon. Throughly satisfyed I went to the dormitory. By the way I bought the plate from the stands by the gangplank.

Later on we got off again and got on the tour busses. they drove us through the hilly country until we came to Athens. We went to a hill across form the Acropolis where I got some pretty good pictures. My girlfriend and I went back to the bus earlier than the rest. We told the guide that we liked Egypt better, so far, and she told us that we were very lucky to be born Americans so that we could see different places and all. Not until later did I understand and appreciate what she said.

Then we went on to the Acropolis. What I liked best were the wine girls holding up the ceiling. Boy was it hard climbing! We saw the Greek theater and the parthenon and all of the temples. I still wonder how all of those building are still standing! We had to get tickets to go up on the Acropolis.

Then we went to the Palace in Athens, which is a copy of Buckingham Palace, and saw the Guards. They have to stand still a whole hour. But if they get tired they march up and down making noises with their guns and shoes. They wore short skirts, leotards, slippers with little tassels, and a hat with a long tassels. My picture of him are just a blur, I am sorry to say.

After that we drove through Athens and back to the ship. Boy was that a full day!

11th day

Nothing unusual happened today but we had a regular class day. I went up to the bow of the boat and saw a bunch of flying fish! They just leaped up and went back into the water. My friends and I played a round of table tennis. I watched a game of deck hockey too! I went to the dance tonight, but it wasn't very good and I left early because it was so hot and crowded. I didn't go to supper tonight because I wasn't about to try to get through that crowd. I showered and went to bed. Good-Night

12th Day

Today all of the classes were shortened and we returned to Benghazi. We couldn't get in to dock so the poor British kids had to get off in life boats! It was awful! It was such a pretty port in Benghazi. We left as soon as the lifeboats got back so we coulet back to Tripoli in good time. The rest of the day we hung around on the top deck. Some of the kids were getting seasick because we were going against the waves. It was so nice sitting out there in the sunshine. It was a pretty boring afternoon. I went to a movie, but left because it was awful. Good-Night

13th Day

Today is the day!!!!!!! We arrived in Tripoli harbor in the afternoon. We got to the dock reserved for us, but we found that we had only room for about a third of the ship! So they put up a make shift gangway. There was a bunch of people waiting for us but our parents were to meet us at the base gate. I rushed through supper. Then we went to our muster station with all of our luggage. Our group was one of the first to get off. It was awful scarry getting down that wobbly gangway with a lose rope for sides. I dropped my sweater but a lady picked it up for me. We got on the bus and drove through Tripoli until we got to the gate. I was really sweating but then I saw Mom and Dad."

Jan sent this to Grandpa Dorsey and he was very impressed, I still am impressed for a twelve year old girl to have made such good notes of her trip that she will remember all her lifetime.

Nancy and I went with a Sunday School group to Germany for ten days. Nancy had a Phaff sewing machine we bought in Germany in 1957 that needed service and repairs. So we took it with us to be repaired while we were there. We landed at Neubiberg, my previous station in Germany, pretty late at night. A small bus was waiting for the group to take them to Berchtesgaden when we landed. Bob and Joan Brooding decided to stay in Munich with us that night so we could take the sewing machine in town the next day to get it repaired. It just so happened that Octoberfest was in full swing and accommodations were hard to get. To our delight the German air force duty officer, found two inns that had room for us. We spent the night at Frau Braun's gasthaus and made reservations for rooms after the conference was over. The next day we went to Berchtesgaden by train. Everyone had a great time at the conference, and had time to take tours to Salzburg, Austria, the salt mines, and Hitler's Eagles Nest high in the Alps.

We took a bus up to the Eagles Nest on a one lane road. The driver had one eye, and the bus came close to the edge of the cliff, which was pretty hairy. After our tour of the Eagles Nest, Nancy, Bob and Joan decided not to ride the bus down the mountain to our hotel, the General Patton. I decided to take the bus, and waved to them as they started the long trek down the steep path. Needless to say I had a good nap at the hotel before they got back. That night and the next day all three were pretty sore and stiff from their walk.

After the conference, everyone stayed in Innsbruck except the Broodings and the Livelys. We took the train back to Munich, checked in at Frau Braun's, and rented a Volkswagen for transportation around the area. During the next three days, Nancy and I saw our maid, Margaret. We took in the Oktoberfest, visited Dachau concentration camp, toured Nymphenburg Palace, and had a great time. The rest of the group returned to Munich on the day we were to return to Wheels

The Base C-54 that was to take us back to Wheelus had a problem before takeoff. One of the pilots told us that it was going to be interesting because one of the four engines had a defective starter and they would try to air start it on the runway. We started down the runway and threw on the brakes halfway to the end. They turned the plane around and tried it again, but the engine would not start. They did this two more times before they pulled back to the ramp where they finally got a new starter put on the engine. The flight home was uneventful, except that Bob Brooding and I, waxed a couple of the pilots who were not flying the plane in a couple of bridge games. I think they thought we were cheating, but Bob and I knew what each other would do since we had been partners many times.

When we arrived back at Wheelus, Jerry Solecki and Gordon Frey, who stayed with the boys while we were gone, said everything went well except when the gold fish showed up in the kitchen sink. Mike and Len told them not to worry about that since it happened before. Jan stayed with the Sanders while we were gone and I don't think they had any trouble.

In May, 1967, Nancy's grandfather Fay Dorsey became deathly ill from cancer. Nancy wanted to return home before he died, but her uncle, Jim Dorsey, told the Red Cross that she was not needed and should not be sent home. We decided that she should get home, so we booked passage on TWA. She returned in time to see him before he died and thinks that he recognized her. She stayed until after the funeral. While Nancy was back in the States, the kids and I moved from Sukel Juma to a five room villa on the base. It took us over two years to get base housing.

Nancy returned to Wheelus around the first of June. The first thing she asked me was when we were going to be evacuated because of the trouble between Israel and the United Arab Republic. This was news to me because no one told us that war was about to occur. On June 6, 1967 the Six Day War began. Israel caught the Egyptian air force on the ground and destroyed it. Gamal Abdel Nasser, Egypt's Prime Minister, broadcast that the U.S. had flown high cover for the Israeli jets and the U.S. aircraft came from Wheelus. Actually, when the war started all USAFE planes at Wheelus returned immediately to Europe.

The local Arabs went berserk. They walked off the base in droves. Some, who worked for Americans as houseboys and employees at the base went into hiding for their lives. American military families as well as other Europeans left their villas and came on base as quickly as they could. They were quartered in the Airman's barracks and other quarters until they were flown to the Continent during the next three days. We had four families staying with us during this time until they were evacuated. Across the street from our villa, a contingent of army engineers camped out in their tents. They set up machine-gun emplacements facing the gate that was about fifty yards from our front door.

At about 7:00 P.M, on the fourth day, June 9, about 6,000 civilians had been evacuated and Col. White made an announcement on the local TV that the worst had past and the majority of the civilians had been evacuated. About one hour later a pipe bomb exploded, at a metal building about thirty yards from the back of our villa. I got Nancy and the kids in the car and took them to Col. Neil Meurlins quarters further back from the wall around the base. Neil's boys returned to our villa, climbed a ladder to its top and looked over the wall to see where the action was. It wasn't too much later that a second pipe bomb exploded at the gate in front of our villa and close to where the army engineers were camped. On a piece of cardboard Jan wrote the following," Dear People, I am in Tripoli, Libya during the Middle East crises. It is very exciting. We are being evacuated to Spain and then home by Mickey Mouses. I have had several people staying at my house since this thing started. We will leave after the Oil people have. Love, Jan"

At four the next morning, we got word that Nancy and the kids could be evacuated. I took them to the flight line where they got a C-5A. Before I kissed them and sent them off, I told them to hop on the first available flight back to the States and I would see them when my tour was over. On their flight to Spain, the flight crew took the children up to the cockpit for a visit. They spent the night at Torehon Airbase in Spain and left the next day on a TWA flight to McGuire AFB, New Jersey. From there they visited Nancy's sister Linda and Billy Gaw who were stationed in New

Jersey. They finally went to Nashville where they lived with Jessie Dorsey until I returned stateside in October.

I stayed at the villa with Bob Brooding and a couple of other officers for the next month. During that time a couple more pipe bombs landed pretty close to my bedroom window. The wall was three feet thick, but I decided to move to the other side of the house. During this time, Col. Hinkle, the Regional Auditor General came to Wheelus for a visit. He spent the night at my house so I let him use my original bed, but no pipe bombs were thrown that night.

We had a Regional Audit Conference in Berlin before I returned home so I took a C-124, from Wheelus to Rhine Main AFB, Germany. We were supposed to leave Wheelus at 9:00 P.M. but number one engine had a leaking oil seal that had to be replaced. We finally took off at 4:00 a.m. and about 45 minutes later the crew chief punched me on the arm and pointed out the right window. The number 4 engine had been feathered and we made a turn to go back to Wheelus. Soon they made another turn and the crew chief told me they decided to put down in Malta which was closer. We had much equipment on this double Decker plane plus 85 army troops that were the engineers at Wheelus. Just about the time the wheels were to hit the ground, the three remaining engines were gunned and we went around for another try at landing. I think because of sun problems at day break the pilots realized that they were lined up on the taxiway rather than on the runway. We made it the second time, but blew out half of the 24 sparkplugs on one of the remaining three good engines. I talked to the crew a month or so later and they told me that when the engines were repaired, they lost another engine on their way to Spain.

While in Malta, I visited Valleta with a couple of Army lieutenants. We got word that another C-124 would be in that evening and we had to be on board by 5:00 A.M. the next morning. The lieutenants had 85 GIs loose in Valletta, and needed to get them rounded up before take off. Valletta was a nice town but was a Navy town and had a strip as wide as an alley where at least 50 whore houses and numerous bars were located. Needless to say we had a hard time rounding up the troops to get them back to the Airport in time for their flight.

The conference in Berlin was great. We took the train from Frankfurt to Berlin through the Russian sector. While in Berlin we stayed at Templehof Airport. I saw where Hitler died, visited Checkpoint Charlie, visited both East and West Berlin (what a difference), and played golf near the Berlin wall. You didn't go after lost balls over the wall. It was a good break from Wheelus. Previously, I had attended another conference in Garmisch, Germany and had been able to spend the night with Roy Newman who worked with me at Kincheloe AFB, Michigan. So during my 2 1/2 year stay at Wheelus I got out to civilization in Germany three times.

I do not have much love for the Libyans. They treat their wives and female children horribly. Women are forced to cover up with a sheet when they are in public and the girls are made to marry when they are 12 or 13. Flies covered Libyan's skin and clothes because the flies were sacred and pollinated the date trees. Thus, a Libyan would not take the time to brush them off or kill them. Because of the flies, many children's eyes were infected. Their sanitary practices were horrendous. I was told never to touch a Libyan's left hand because toilet tissue was never used.

My first encounter with the local Libyans was the day my family arrived. We moved into a villa in Sulka Juma and the movers came with our household goods. Before we left the States two movers packed and placed all our furniture in a van in 4 to 5 hours. Our truck of furniture, etc. arrived at our villa with about 10 workers and a truck driver. The truck driver immediately lay down on our porch until it was his time to make tea. The ten workers took the whole day to unpack our household goods and move them into the villa. In one instance, six of the workers tried to assemble the baby bed with no success. To my amazement very little damage had occurred during the move.

During our first night in the villa, drums were beating, and horns started blowing outside our door. Donkeys and camels were braying, bells were ringing, Arabs were chanting, and cars were racing up and down the street in front of our house. Nancy and the children felt threatened, but we found out the next day that a wedding was taking place. Arabs were called to prayer at 5:00 A.M. each morning and the chanting over a loud speaker began at a mosque next door. This noise carried on the entire time we were in Libya, so we got used to it.

Once, Nancy was bartering with an Arab in the old town of Tripoli over the price of a sheep skin. The seller got mad when Nancy walked away and ran after her shouting--Damn, damn, damn. He finally relented, and she bought the sheep skin for a reasonable price.

Once when we took a sight seeing ride along the Sea, a bus kept passing us and tried to run us off the road three or four times. He would pass us then slow to a near stop until we passed, then he would try to run us off the road again. We did not make many trips in the country after that.

Don't ever be reincarnated as a donkey in Libya. Coming from work I passed a Libyan with a donkey pulling a small cart with a camel in it. The Arab was beating it with a two by four board to keep the cart moving. On another day we had to stop the car to let a herd of sheep and their drovers pass by. This same occurrence looked as if it could have happened 2000 year ago. If you passed by the Sukel Juma's market place, you would always see a camel's head and its bloody neck hanging outside the shop.

These everyday happenings, tremendous heat from ghiblis, and the attitudes of the Libyans prompted me to be ready to leave that place when my time was up. I did not want to stay one minute longer than I had too.

I received orders to Barksdale AFB, Louisiana and was to report there in October 1967. Was I ready to leave Wheelus! The group gave Jim Baker and me a going away party the night before I left. I drank one cream de menthe and watched the rest of the people get smashed. Brooding told the Air Police to stay away from the BOQ even though they would probably get calls for the disturbance.

The next morning, Jim and I boarded the Freedom Bird for the good old USA. As the wheels left the ground cheers abounded all over the plane. There are many other things I remember about Wheelus: the job we did, the people we worked and played with, the Arabs and their peculiar ways, the heat, the sand, and most of all -- leaving it all behind.

CHAPTER 7

October 1967 - March 1970

Barksdale AFB Bossier City, Louisiana

Upon return to the States, Nancy met me at the Nashville airport. We spent the night in a hotel downtown and celebrated my homecoming. After four months of separation we had a lot to celebrate. Early the next morning we went to Jessie's home where Nancy and the children had been staying after they were evacuated from Wheelus. For the next couple of weeks we spent time in Nashville and visited Mom and Jim in Kentucky.

In November, we moved to Bossier City, LA and bought a new house in a subdivision just south of Barksdale AFB. I could drive to my office in five minutes from our new home. It was two stories, had three bedrooms and a bath upstairs for the children, an open balcony and stairs down to a large den, dining area and kitchen. Also, downstairs we had our bedroom and bath, an entrance hall, and a large living room plus a two car garage. This was the first house we really owned and loved it.

Jan, Mike and Len got settled in school and we only had Billy still at home. They made friends easily and adjusted to their new environment very quickly as they always did. Our neighbors were mostly Air Force families who made us welcome. That was what we always loved about Air Force life, everyone was usually in a transit state because you would never know where or when you would be moving next. Thus, most of the folks were very friendly and we made the best friends of our lives with them.

One afternoon Jan and a few of her friends gathered in our living room and had a séance party around the coffee table. They had the drapes drawn and the lights out so it was pretty dark. They didn't know I was home so I went into our bedroom closet next to the living room and cried out an eerie BOOOOO.. All of them screamed and were out the front door in less than ten seconds. Mike tried to throw an egg out of Jan's bedroom window toward a neighbors house because their kids had egged our car earlier. He missed the window and splashed the egg on the side of the wall. He had a hard time explaining this and had a harder time trying to scrub the mess off the wall. Len had a fire cracker go off in his hand on the Fourth of July and ended up at the emergency room. Billy won an Easter bunny at the Officers Club and slept with it for a long time. Nancy burned her hands so badly chopping hot green peppers that she had to go to the emergency room for treatment. Jan became a volunteer for a head start class on base and, while there, decided that she wanted to be a teacher and have a career in education. Nancy became involved with the activities of the Officer's Wives Club and she and I started teaching the youth group Sunday School class at the base Chapel.

I drove the family to Colorado Springs, Colorado for a week conference of the Central and Western Regional Auditor General Divisions. The headquarters officials and key personnel of each region's resident auditor offices were present. As we were checking into the hotel, we heard the alarm bell of the nearby elevators go off. The elevator doors opened and there stood Mike and Len. So my family made a name for itself within the first hour of our arrival.

Lots of old friends from the past were there. Nancy and I played liars dice with Elroy Wells and Bob Storrs from Scott AFB. A light burned out over the table so Bob climbed up on a chair, took off the globe which he immediately dropped and shattered. We cleaned up the mess and carried on with our game. Bob, who was in his early forties, died a few months after this meeting. I've always missed this true friend.

Nancy and the children saw all the sights around Colorado Springs. We toured the Air Force Academy and was really impressed with the Chapel also visited Elsie Fults, who had remained in Colorado Springs while Jim was on tour in Viet Nam. We drove up Cheyenne Mountain and on our way down burned out the brakes of our new Pontiac station wagon, the first of many calamities with this lemon.

With my Air Force group, I toured the NORAD command facility deep beneath Cheyenne Mountain and spent one afternoon at the Air Force Academy. Most of the remaining time was spent in meetings at our Colorado Springs hotel. We still have a lot of camera slides of the trip.

I also attended a meeting at Norton AFB located near San Bernadino, California. This week consisted mainly of meetings concerning audit procedures and other Air Force business. I had to take a commercial helicopter from Los Angeles to San Bernadino. Two weeks prior to my flight one of these helicopters crashed and two or three weeks after I left California another one was lost. The company went out of business after these catastrophes.

During our time at Barksdale we took several trips to Nashville and Kentucky. We went to Washington D.C. to see the Hill's and the Brooding's and toured all the museums and other places of interest for a week. While in Washington, I developed an abscessed cyst on my tail bone. This had occurred several times over the prior years and had been lanced each time by a military doctor. This time I went to Fort Belvoire and an enlisted medic cut the whole thing out. I have never had that problem again.

Nancy and I spent a couple of days in San Antonio reviewing my service records. Soon after we returned from San Antonio, the entire family went to New Orleans for a long weekend. We stayed with the Kimball's and their four children. Ed, Marilyn, Nancy and I ate at Antoines and a restaurant on the west bank of the Mississippi the next evening. While at the latter restaurant, John Unitas returned a call I made to him. One of Ed's kids took the call and she could hardly believe John had called and was almost speechless. I got in touch with John and he invited the Kimball family and our gang to his hotel room the next morning before the Baltimore Colts played the New Orleans Saints. The twelve of us went to his hotel room and visited with John and his roommate Earl Morral for about a half an hour. We got their autographs and took several pictures. That afternoon we went to the game which the Colts won. After we returned to Barksdale, I opened the camera and found that I had no film in it, so I lost all the shots I took in San Antonio and of John and Earl in New Orleans.

When I started my tour at Barksdale in November 1967, I settled in at the office with the following staff: the assistant resident auditor was GS-12 Mildred Engle; auditors were Captain Roger Monteyene, Lieutenant John Davis, Senior Master Sergeant Earl DeLozier; and secretary was Marilyn Graves.

Millie Engle was well qualified and was a truly loyal person. She took care of cost reduction items at the Base and 2nd Air Force Command levels. Millie helped supervise the auditors but mainly left that responsibility to me. If my name was going to be signed on reports of audit, I wanted to know what was in them, how they were supported by working papers, how they were written and how they were received by those we were auditing. I never forgot the slogan, "Be right before you write." I remained friends with Millie and we exchanged Christmas cards for years.

John Davis was an excellent young auditor and his work was outstanding. Nancy and Brenda Davis became close friends and remained that way over the years. Several of his audits had significant findings which were corrected to the benefit of the Air Force and the success of our small office. John was transferred to Viet Nam for a year, then decided to take the CPA exam which he passed, resigned his regular commission and obtained a position with an oil pipeline company in Houston, Texas. Through the years, John has been a success and is currently CEO of the Mobile, Alabama Gas Company.

Roger Monteyene was one of the most intriguing individuals I ever met. He was a likable person but had a lot of strange quirks. He drove an old Mercedes sedan that had bald tires which went flat or blew out every week or so. He owned a female Afghan hound dog which he wanted to breed, but could not find a mate. One day he came in the office and said that he bought another Afghan. In the next breath he said his new dog was also female. One day John, Roger and I were walking from the sandwich bar when a young airman with his right arm in a sling passed us without saluting. Roger jumped on the airman, so I intervened and told the airman to forget it and proceed where he was going. In another instance, Roger built a "hate fence" of tree limbs and brush between his and the neighbor's house because they had a falling out. Roger kept a chart of all the stocks he invested in, but if anyone said off hand that a certain stock looked good, Roger would pick up the phone and buy several shares of it. Roger is probably a multimillionaire now.

Earl DeLozier was a dependable and loyal person who always did a great job, especially auditing supply, aircraft maintenance and procurement activities. Results of his work and techniques he developed were later successfully used by other Air Force base auditors. Several years later, I visited Earl and his wife in Albuquerque, New Mexico. We had dinner at Poncho's Mexican Buffet and after the meal they took me to a jewelry dealer where I bought a beautiful silver and turquoise necklace for Nancy. It is still one of her favorites.

I had two responsibilities at Barksdale: Liaison Auditor for 2nd Air Force and its twelve SAC bases and Wings located in central United States; and audit of the 2nd Bomb Wing at Barksdale. Instead of performing audits myself I left the audit work to my staff and concentrated on supervising and issuing local (2nd Bomb Wing) reports of audit. I missed doing some of the detailed work, but enjoyed my liaison work with 2nd Air Force officials.

We issued audit reports at the local level that resulted in changes in procedures Air Force wide. For example, we noted that maintenance part packages designated for specific B-52 bombers and C-135 refueling tanker aircraft were being sent to the bases where those aircraft were supposedly stationed. In many instances the planes had been deployed to the Pacific area for operations in the Viet Nam war. As a result, needed and often critical maintenance was delayed or not made. Our solution was to notify the depots that sent the packages to keep an accurate update of where the specific planes were so the parts could be forwarded readily to the actual locations of the planes.

In one audit we noted that the supply and maintenance organizations did not coordinate properly when supplies were requisitioned. As a result needless paperwork and excess supplies were transferred when they shouldn't have been and aircraft that may be needed for the war effort were not operationally ready because of supposedly lack of parts. Our report stated that maintenance and supply personnel did not work in harmony. Not long after we issued this report, Headquarters SAC Inspector General officials arrived for an operational readiness inspection (ORI). One inspector whom I had known when he inspected conditions at Wheelus picked up this report and found that nothing had been done to correct the problem. To my surprise, he asked me to attend their final discussion of findings. I attended and found my chair at the head table (I really wanted to be inconspicuous). After the meeting Col.. Rafalco, the Wing Commander, asked me to attend a meeting in his office with the directors of supply and maintenance. He asked me a few questions about this discrepancy and I told him our position. When I left his office I imagine he had quite a heated discussion with the two officers.

One other time Col. Rafalco asked me to come to his office as he was concerned about cost reduction actions for the Wing. He stated that his people could not get many cost reduction items through our audit review process and approved. He further stated that this could affect his career since his efficiency reports contained a section on meeting cost reduction goals. I told Col Rafalco that many of his submissions did not really save the government any money. I suggested that he have his cost reduction official come over to our audit office and review the submissions we had received from other bases that Millie had to review for approval. When his person come over and reviewed other submissions, suddenly 2nd Bomb Wing cost reduction reached and exceeded their goals.

An Audit Headquarters visit to our office reported that, "This is an excellent AGRO (Auditor General Resident Office) operation which is managed exceedingly well. The AGRO/base relations are outstanding and the staff is very well qualified."

I really appreciated the 2nd Air Force officials that I worked with to coordinate audit and base relationships. With these officials, I was able to help Chief Master Sergeant Jack Rash, my old friend from Neuibiberg Germany, to be transferred to Barksdale for his final assignment before he retired. The Lt. Col who was in charge of the 2nd Air Force cost reductions helped me get Jack transferred. This officer had the additional responsibility of coordinating the movement of Presidential limousines and other vehicles to locations that the President visited.

Major Bobby Presley, the Deputy Comptroller of 2nd AF, was the officer I dealt closely with and will always respect. He knew how important audits were to the Air Force mission and called on me to clear up several misunderstandings and give verbal and written presentations to comptroller personnel within the Command. He finished his career as a major general. Three different times he offered me jobs with his organizations.

Bobby and I worked together to clear up a dispute at one of the bases. The civil engineer at this base in northern Indiana cut off the power to the resident auditor's family quarters in the middle of the winter because of their dispute over cost reduction denials and a Party involving gambling at the local officers club. As a result both officers were transferred to other bases. Major Presley was responsible for the following letter from Lt. Gen. David C. Jones

"Subject: Relationship Between Commander and Staff With Resident Auditor--Dated 15 September 1969

1. A recent incident at a base in the command disclosed a situation where the relationship between the commanders and their staffs with the resident auditor had deteriorated to a point where neither could function effectively in their areas of mutual interest. In such a situation, the Air Force is the loser.

2. Air Force Manual 170-6, paragraphs 20630 and 70631, outlines the relationship of the commander and his staff with the resident auditor. This manual encourages the exchange of information, ideas, and advice. Despite the fact that the auditor is directly responsible to the Auditor General rather than the local commander, the commander should always consider him as a member of his staff and strive to develop a harmonious and cooperative relationship with him. When this is done, you will find that the auditor can be one of the most valuable men on your staff. As a result of his activities throughout the entire unit, he frequently can pinpoint actual or potential problem areas soon enough to permit you to take corrective action. In addition to his audit functions, he should be used as a consultant in such matters as improved financial management, interpretation of new or revised directives, accounting and related financial aspects of contract negotiations and settlements or for any other purpose your feel advisable.

3. You should review the provisions of these paragraphs in AFM 170-6 and act accordingly. In the event the rapport implied cannot be achieved and difficulties arise, this headquarters should be advised so that differences may be resolved in conjunction with the Second Air Force Liaison Auditor.

David C. Jones, Lt Gen, USAF
Commander"

Additionally; on March 6, 1970, the following letter was sent to the Auditor General.

"Subject: Resident Auditors

Major General George F. Brown
USAF Auditor General
Norton AFB, CA 92409

1. During visits to bases of the command, I make it a point to stop and visit the Resident Auditors. I have been highly impressed with the caliber of people in your organization and the high quality of their audits. Since the best of audit findings are of little value if not used, I stress to my commanders that they should always consider the Resident Auditors as

members of their staffs and strive to develop harmonious and cooperative relationships with them.

2. I take this opportunity of expressing my appreciation to all Resident Auditors of Second Air Force bases. I am proud of the professional manner in which they perform their duties and am pleased with their products.

David C. Jones, Lt Gen, USAF
Commander"

General Jones retired from service as the Chairman of the Joint Chiefs of Staff. Everywhere he went he took Bobby Presley with him. They made a great team.

In the fall of 1968 I was advised that I had been passed over for permanent major. Several other auditors fared the same fate. The next year I was passed over again, so I could either be down graded to an airman first rank, join the inactive reserves as a major, or be honorably discharged and receive a $15,000 severance pay. I chose the latter since my children would be graduating from high school soon and the severance pay would come in handy.

This was the lowest point in my life because I loved the Air Force and at age 40, I hated to start all over in the civilian ranks. I recorded my thoughts in a letter to a US Senator with as copy to the Air Force Chief of Staff. A part of this letter reads: "Four Regular Air Force Officer auditors and I were passed over for the second time to the rank of Permanent Major. This passover eliminated us from the Air Force, thereby causing us to lose our military retirement benefits. We occupy responsible positions, and I believe the other auditors have performed as well as I have. Otherwise, we would not have been designated the positions we are presently occupying. A total of 3663 officers were considered, and 3506 were promoted (95,7%). Only 14 auditors were promoted out of 21 considered (66.6%). Further, Auditor General personnel have suffered greatly on other promotion boards in the past few years. It is inconceivable to me that auditors, whom I honestly believe are an elite hand picked group of Comptroller personnel should not receive their just promotions."

I received a letter from the Assistant Vice Chief of Staff trying to explain the reasoning of Auditor General personnel lack of promotions but he failed to justify his position to me. On January 14, 1970 the Air Force Times had an article entitled "Radical changes to OER studied which could affect how promotion boards evaluated personnel when they are eligible for promotion". I never learned how that turned out.

I prepared resumes and civil service documents for government employment and received letters from several companies. I had interviews with ARMCO and Genesco officials in Dayton, OH and Nashville, TN soon after leaving service. David Jones, CEO of Humana gave my name to Kentucky Fried Chicken officers and I talked with them a few times but could never see them officially. Major Presley offered me a job at Little Rock AFB with the base exchange system as a GS 11. I thought I could do better elsewhere so I turned that down.

Also; I sent letters to past associates and friends telling them of my plight and seeking advise and asking if they would be references that I could give possible employers. Their response was all I could ask for and I will always be thankful to them. General Bill Evan's "Letter of Evaluation"," included in Chapter 6, was instrumental when I met with Agriculture's OIG official, Bill Dickson in Washington

Some other comments from friends and associates follow:

Col Joe White, Wing Commander, Wheelus AB, Libya--Got your letter this week end and was glad to hear from you but surprised as hell to find out about your situation. Can't figure out what could have happened but the service always seems to screw up just at the wrong time. As far as I am concerned you are one of the finest guys I've known in the service.---You may not have heard that Col George Dorman was killed a short while ago in Viet-Nam. What a hell of a way to go. Be glad that you are getting out Bill, and let me know what I can do for you.

Col. R. A. Bosworth, Commander 301ˢᵗ Air Refueling Wing--Sorry to hear of your plight and I agree 100% that it was undeserved. I enjoyed my contacts with you at Barksdale and always thought that you did a bang-up job.

Jack Craf, the dean of University of Louisville Business School wrote me a nice letter and strongly advised that I continue in Government service since I already had 15 years invested toward retirement. Many others were also supportive and said many nice things to me.

On March 31, 1970, the day I left service, I received my second Commendation Medal (First Oak Leaf Cluster) for Meritorious Service at Barksdale. The General presenting me the certificate and medal wanted the medal back and told me that I could get one at the base exchange. I kept the nice certificate but did not purchase the medal since I already had one and could not go into the exchange since I had turned in my ID card.

We left Barksdale and returned to Nashville where we rented a house while I hunted for a new job in the cold cruel world.

CHAPTER 8

April 1970 - September 1973

Washington, D.C.

During the first week in April, I moved the family to Nashville. We rented a house close to Linda and Jessie, got the kids entered into school and settled in trying to find employment somewhere in the USA. I contacted several Federal Agencies and got positive feedback from the U.S. Department of Agriculture Regional Office of Inspector General (OIG) office in Hyattsville, Maryland. A week later, I received a phone call from a retired Air Force Officer who worked at OIGs Headquarters in Washington. He related that I should come to Washington as soon as possible and interview for a job at the headquarters and I should talk with a Mr. Bill Dickson. The next day, I hopped on a plane and saw the cherry blossoms in full bloom (a good luck sign), just before landing at National Airport, spent the night with Ken and Betsy Hill, then went downtown the next morning for my interview.

I could tell that Bill Dickson was the right person for me to talk to. He was a gentleman, later stated that he was impressed with General Evan's evaluation, and wanted me to come to work for him at the Headquarters in Washington. While there the Regional Inspector General (RIG) at Hyattsville intervened and said that I should be assigned to his regional office since I had contacted them first. So it was decided that I would be hired as a GS 12 auditor and work out of the Region II Hyattsville office. As it worked out, this arrangement was the best thing that could happen to me.

For the next couple of months I stayed with Ken and Betsy Hill and Bob and Joan Brooding. During this period Nancy came up for a short stay and we bought a house in Mount Vernon about a half a mile from George Washington's home. It was a four bedroom, three bathroom split foyer brick and shake house. There was plenty of room for the family, Bootsie (our dog from Africa) and other pets. We had lots of trees in the yard and lived there comfortably for three years.

We were close to the Hill's, Brooding's and Stark and Peg Sanders. The family moved in June and quickly settled in as they always did. Jan and Mike could walk to the high school two blocks away and Len and Billy could walk to their school not far away. During our three years in Mount Vernon, Jan and Mike graduated and both had their commencements at Constitution Hall in Washington and their baccalaureates at the National Cathedral. Jan left us to begin college at George Peabody in Nashville and earned her degree in Special Education. Mike graduated just before we left Washington and went with us to our new assignment in New Orleans in 1973. Len and Billy continued in school in the area until we moved to Louisiana.

We really enjoyed our stay in the Washington area as we had our friends and loved the attractions such as concerts, museums, great dining, little league activities and the fellowship we enjoyed at the Old Presbyterian Meeting House in downtown Alexandria, Virginia. Nancy and I joined the choir and loved it. Jan, Mike and Len would often skip out of Sunday School and walk a couple of blocks to our favorite ice cream parlor on King Street.

Jan and Mike both got jobs during the summer and after school. Len played little league football and I coached his team. They were pretty good and won several games. Mike and Len delivered the Washington Post newspaper for quite a while and Billy was growing up very quickly. Those three years sped by.

My commute from home to the regional office was north up the George Washington Parkway, across the Potomac River, north on the eastern side of the river to Hyattsville, Maryland, about twenty five miles. I shared a ride with Jimmie McDonald and Frank Reynolds much of the time. Both became great friends and have since passed away.

Frank smoked too much and died in his forties from lung disease. He weighed all of a hundred pounds, was about five-two and had a drinking problem. The inside of his Volkswagen windshield was stained thick from his cigarette smoke. He was a very smart person who knew the ins and outs of auditing and had a knack of communicating orally and in writing effectively. His problem was the bottle, and he continued to stay in trouble all the time I knew him. Some of his escapades were legendary. I think he bought, lived in and sold three homes during the three years we worked together. He was a rascal but I loved him.

Jimmie McDonald worked off and on with me for my fifteen years with OIG and was my boss for eight years in the Southeast Region. He was a character too and I will mention him many times in this and forthcoming chapters.

Soon after I started to work at the regional office the RIG and his Assistant Regional Inspector General (ARIG) transferred to the Atlanta Regional Office. Charles Bremmer and John Means replaced them. They were both good administrators and persons that were easy to work with. I had great relationships with all of my bosses and coworkers. My favorites besides Frank and Jimmie, noted above, were: Charles Riser, who would later be my RIG in Atlanta; Joe Fisch; Hubie Sparks; Arnold Stultz; Carl Momberger and several others in Washington Headquarters.

I was in "hog heaven" since I would be doing the audits myself and would not have to supervise a bunch of people. I was told to learn the Food Stamp Program and would be working with another GS 12 auditor, Frank Fetzer, on the municipal Washington DC Food Stamp Program.

Since the ARIG that I was assigned to was leaving for Atlanta, Bill Dickson who interviewed me would be the head honcho of the audit and Frank and I would receive directions from him. After a week of learning about the Food Stamp Program, Frank Fetzer and I, with Bill Dickson, had an entrance conference with the local Washington DC Food Stamp Program officials. My work in the Food Stamp Program in Washington and various Maryland State and local offices follow.

USDA Food Stamp Program
Washington, DC

The Food Stamp Program (FSP) is managed by each state and funded by the federal government; therefore, federal auditors had the audit responsibility over how the program was managed. I found that food stamps were very beneficial to those in need and worthwhile. However; in a few instances that the program was abused, the media and many critics complained when discrepancies were noted. Only about 5 to 10 percent of questionable abuses occurred but when 114,000 Washington food stamp recipients received $3.1 million in food stamps per month, losses would be substantial. At this time recipients would pay cash for their stamps based on their income and the cash received would be deposited into the Federal Reserve Banks around the country. Thus Frank and I split our audit tests into two parts. Frank would audit cash accountability and I would audit the certification and issuance of stamps to the recipients.

There were 13 certification centers in the city and 54 issuing offices where the recipients would pay for and receive their stamps. When a person was approved and certified for stamps the recipient's name and case number assigned were entered into the central computer system at the main office. Monthly, the computer would produce authorization to purchase cards (pre-punched computer punch cards) and send them to the approved recipient. Upon receipt, the recipient would take the authorization to purchase card (ATP) to an issuing office and receive stamps. If an applicant was destitute and needed food stamps immediately the certification center worker would manually punch an ATP and give it to the recipient so that he could take it to an issuing office and receive stamps.

Washington Food Stamp Office officials believed that the program was being abused because about 4,000 manually punched ATPs were being issued each month and their 13 certification centers were being overrun by people wanting food stamps. Thus they requested the audit.

Soon after we started the audit I walked into a file room and noticed several stacks of computer printouts stacked around the room. I asked what they were used for and was told that if a person did not receive his ATP the printout would be researched so that they could manually issue another card to the individual. The printouts were prepared in case number order. After I considered this, I went to the computer programmer and asked him if he would prepare me a monthly printout in alphabetical order and another one in street address sequence He said he could and got them to me in short order. The printouts showing ATP transactions were quite large since about 25,000 households were shown.

As a result of my reviewing these two printouts and comparing the recipients' signatures on the backs of ATPs, I found many questionable conditions that were reported in our audit as follows:

"We requested and obtained from Data Services Division two special computer listings showing names and addresses of all recipients who negotiated ATP's in June 1970. One computer listing categorized the names of recipients in alphabetical order and the other listing showed the addresses of the same individuals in street number sequence. We traced the recipients shown on these listings to the ATP's negotiated in June. In 738 instances, recipients negotiated two or more ATP's in June causing USDA to lose about $47,800, the bonus value of the erroneous food stamp issuances. Based on the June loss and the fact that the number of eligible households are increasing significantly, USDA may lose over $600,000 in Fiscal Year 1971 unless SSA promptly initiates procedures to eliminate duplicate ATP issuances. It is also significant to note that 36 of the recipients cashed from three to six ATP's in June."

This was the first time this procedure of reviewing sequenced printouts was used by USDA auditors and was continually used until most audit responsibilities were turned over to the State agencies in the 1980s. I thank my old Memphis boss Pete Moretta for telling me to use the computer as much as possible when conducting audits.

Frank Fetzer found that one issuing agent owed USDA more than $106,000 for funds collected and not deposited and found seven other serious conditions during our audit that required correction. To The State Agency's credit, they took immediate action to upgrade their computer program to eliminate recipients cashing multiple ATP cards. They stopped manually issuing ATPs but ran recipient applications through the computer in the overnight hours to eliminate the duplications then mailed the correct ones out the next morning.

When the State Agency changed their issuance procedures, all hell broke out. The Chairman of the D C Commission on Food, Nutrition and Health sent a telegram to USDA Secretary stating: "On Monday, February 1, a hunger crisis will be created in Washington D.C. if the proposed new system for food stamp certification and issuance is implemented without adequate measure to allow for emergency provision of food stamps during the waiting period. Therefore, after due consultation with community representatives, they demand that there be a delay in implementation of the proposed new system for food stamp certification and issuance until such time as each applicant can be provided with sufficient food stamps to prevent hunger during the waiting periods"

According to a Washington Star article: "A delegation of citizens and the Mayor's Commission on Food, Nutrition, and Health met with Asst. Secretary of Agriculture Richard E. Lyng challenging the results of an audit last summer that turned up irregularities. Commission member Polly Shackelton, a former city councilwoman, had charged that the report 'impugns the integrity and honesty of every person in the food stamp program'.."

I retained statements out of three congressional records, ten Washington newspaper articles, and memorandums from State Agency and USDA officials concerning this audit. USDA and the State Agency did not back down and I don't think any recipient missed any meals.

Seventeen months after the Washington Office changed their issuance system we performed another audit. Our examination disclosed that in these 17 months, an average of 1,880 less households were issued monthly manual ATPs than in the previous period. The average monthly food stamp costs in 1970 amounted to $307,240; 17 months later the monthly costs averaged $141,995. Thus, USDA saved $2.8 million for the period between the audits.

It was a great pleasure to work for Bill Dickson and with Frank Fetzer. Bill never questioned what I was doing and was very helpful in preparing the audit reports that accurately presented the facts. Also, Frank and I received Certificates of Merit (Cash Awards) for the audit.

Maryland FSP

During the spring and summer of 1971, Arnold Stultz supervised and I was the Auditor in Charge (AIC) of a team of auditors performing audits of Baltimore and several other Maryland county FSP offices. The main thing we found was that erroneous/ fraudulent food stamp issuances were occurring there also. Some of the same people who were getting duplicate stamps in Washington were also getting them at various offices in Maryland. We worked with OIG investigators to determine the extent of these actions.

Since we knew the names of the individuals who had made fraudulent duplicate applications to get stamps in Washington, the investigators put indelible ink on stamps to be issued by the Maryland offices when these people showed up. These individuals would take the stamps to a D.C. grocer and get 50 cents on each dollar value. The grocer in turn would deposit the stamps at his local; bank for face value. Then the bank would deposit these marked stamps with the U. S. Depository in Washington. At this depository OIG investigators took a special light that would pick up the invisible ink on the stamps where they could identify the store that was fencing the stamps.

The Washington Post November 17, 1971 article reported that, "The D.C. grocer and one of his employees were indicted on 67 counts with conspiring to purchase more than $11,000 in fraudulently obtained food stamps from at least four un-indicted coconspirators. The coconspirators allegedly obtained food stamps in 16 Maryland and Virginia cities by using false and fictitious names, addresses, family composition, and former employments." An accompanying article in the paper stated, "the Montgomery Maryland food stamp supervisor said that he traced his problems back to last February. At that time, the District of Columbia changed its regulations and stopped giving out food stamps on demand. Instead, a time delay was instituted during which applications are checked. From that time on, he said, 'on any given day you would see license plates from the District of Columbia in the (Rockville) parking lot. Once he recalled, a social worker gave food stamps to an individual in Bethesda on Wednesday and found the same man in the Rockville two days later, applying for stamps under a different name. The man was turned away'."

I had a home visit with a female food stamp recipient in Snow Hill, Maryland to determine her eligibility for food stamps. She lived in a run down house and appeared to need food stamps so I told her she should continue in the program. Later, when I checked her records at the food stamp office I found that she was obtaining stamps using three different aliases and three other persons she claimed as dependents were also being issued food stamps illegally. She and her confederates had been issued about $5,880 in illegal food stamps. She and her confederates were referred for investigation. I do not know the outcome of this case.

In investigating grocery store management and other individuals who abused this program, OIG investigators used food stamps to buy liquor, furniture, TV sets, an automobile, and even a horse while I was in Washington working with them. I don't know if this type of activity is occurring today, but I expect it is. However, I've not seen much written about it in the local papers.

Since I will turn 78 tomorrow (January 10, 2008) and was in my early 70s when I started writing about our tour at Wheelus, I have decided to abridge the rest of my bio. to only touch on the highlights of my life and not bore the reader of much detail. If I get too long winded the reader should bypass a couple of paragraphs and get to something more interesting. I'm sorry that it has taken so long to compile the above but I am quite a procrastinator when I don't have deadlines to meet. So, if I'm going to get this done before I'm not able or available I better get with it! BILL

In 1972 I was promoted to GS 13, Supervisory auditor. The most significant thing noted in my recommendation for promotion document was that OIG needed to keep me since other agencies would be seeking my services. This was a far cry from the Air Force.

During the time I was doing Food Stamp audits in 1971, I wrote a letter that the Regional Inspector General forwarded to Food and Nutrition Service suggesting that credit cards and corresponding point of sale terminals be used by area post offices to issue food stamps, thus eliminating the ATP cards; to save millions of dollars yearly in their preparation, handling, and postal costs. The postal department had adequate transmission lines so it was feasible. Nothing was done and, at the turn of the century, 2000, the State of Kentucky initiated a credit card system in lieu of food stamps thus saving Federal funds and establishing better control over the issuances. I don't know if other states have initiated such a system or if they are still preparing, issuing and redeeming ATPs. If so, over the past 30 or so years billions of dollars have been wasted.

In another instance I was more successful. During a Farmer's Home Administration (FmHA) audit I noticed that the local FmHA offices received individual's copies of receipts from the Kansas City computer center showing that home loan borrowers had made their monthly payments. I asked the county supervisor what he did with them. He stated that he filed them in each individual's folder and if the receipt had not been received he would contact the borrower and press him for payment. He also stated that the borrower received a duplicate copy of the receipt from the computer center. This had been going on for some time or since the borrowers sent their monthly payments to Kansas City and did not make local payments. I wrote a letter and the Regional Inspector General (RIG) forwarded it to our auditors in Kansas City stating that mailing and handling costs would be almost eliminated if only delinquency notices were sent to the borrowers and county offices. This suggestion was adopted and hundreds of thousands of individual loans were serviced properly and economically.

While at the Northeast Region, I performed and supervised FmHA home loan activity audits and noted many conditions where county officials, contractors or others erecting housing for borrowers failed to meet required housing standards and protect the borrowers or FmHA itself. Some homes were poorly built or not adequate, failed to have safe water or sewage facilities, or did not meet plans and specification requirements.

When I supervised a nation wide audit on Agricultural research and grants to Universities, I experienced my first taste of the bureaucracy at OIG. OIGs department head over this area was about to retire and did not want to make any waves, so he deleted ninety percent of the findings in our thirty five page draft report and prepared a two page letter to the responsible agency. Some of the things deleted were: One University drew all their annual loan/grant funds at the beginning of the year rather than when it was needed as required. They placed the funds received into federal interest bearing accounts, thus the Government was paying interest on its own money. The Agency did not consider other Department's research results. Agriculture was funding Universities for the effects tobacco had on rodents to determine positive health conditions while at the same time the Surgeon General was funding the same research to find harmful effects. Later in my career I would experience similar bureaucratic actions to impinge on the integrity of an audit.

During my third year with the Northeast Region, I was advised that all of USDA's various accounting offices would be merged into the National

Finance Center located in New Orleans. The center in New Orleans already disbursed payroll checks bi-monthly to its hundred thousand employees. Other accounting activity was performed by each of twenty or so agencies (FmHA, FNS, ASCS, etc.). Centralization of these activities into one would be developed at New Orleans. I was directed by OIG to be their representative in planning for this centralization.

During the summer of 1973, OIG suggested that I take a lateral move there and in due time, I would be promoted to GS 14. I would have a staff of seven or eight auditors on sight to audit ongoing operations and monitor the development of new computer programs to control various payment and receipt operations (phone bills, gas credit card expenditures, utility bills, supply and service costs, etc.).

I loved working in and around Washington and was respected by the auditors I supervised and my bosses at the Northeast Region and Headquarters in Washington itself. The Inspector General told me I had a great future with OIG. Bill Dickson, who hired me, was leery of my transfer and offered to let me have audit responsibilities over Agricultural Foreign Trade.

After considering most everything including the welfare of my family, I decided to go to New Orleans. Jan and Mike had graduated from high school and the environment in the Washington area was not the greatest for Billy and Len, still in middle and high school. So, this was the main reason that I decided to accept the transfer. On the first of September 1973 we packed our bags and were off to New Orleans.

CHAPTER 9

September 1973 - May 1976

New Orleans, Louisiana

Prior to leaving Alexandria we gave our dog Bootsie to an elderly couple then drove to Slidell, La. and checked into the Ramada Inn on Labor Day and watched the Jerry Lewis telethon that night. Jan was at school in Nashville and Mike remained in Virginia with a friend and would be with us soon. The next day I went into East New Orleans to the new USDA National Finance Center and met my audit staff of five auditors and a secretary. The first week I visited the Finance Center officials and got settled in the job.

Since Slidell was east of the Finance Center and away from the city, we closed on a new home in Slidell and got Len and Billy in school. The first day Billy came home from school and complained that he had a terrible meal of red beans and rice and was not at all happy about it. Len quickly made new friends and liked his new environment. Mike decided to attend college in New Orleans and work in a fast food restaurant. Our subdivision adjoined a country club and golf course so Nancy and I joined the club and the boys and I could play golf when we wanted.

Our next door neighbors were native Louisianans, Don and Flo Bowman. We became great friends and Don recruited me into the local Kiwanis Club. He was the local juvenile officer working for the Parish court and cared so much for the kids who got in trouble. He was industrious and readily took to Billy. Don's influence had a great deal to do with Billy getting interested in working with wood. Billy, with Don's guidance, made two wooden model oil wells for the school's science fair. One received a first prize award at Slidell but was not considered for a prize in the regional Parish show because the judges felt that someone Billy's age could not build such a model. He did! Both oil well models are in our attic today.

Len had a friend whose dad opened a theatre in downtown Slidell. So, Len went to work selling tickets, candy, and finally running the projectors. He always made friends and for his birthday, I took Len, Billy, and five of Len's buddies to the New Orleans Poncho Mexican Buffet. The restaurant served all the tacos, enchiladas, and other goodies that you could eat when you raised a flag at the table. One kid ate five orders of refried beans! We had an interesting 25 mile trip back to Slidell that night.

On each Fourth of July, Len, Billy, and their buddies engaged in bottle rocket wars with the boys across the street who they usually didn't associate with. The bottle rockets streaked across the sky and made noise and smoke every where. We were lucky that no one ever got hurt. I was there to light the rockets with my usual cigar.

Jan continued her education in Nashville and obtained her degree the year that we left Louisiana. After graduation she started teaching special education in Hazard, KY for a year before returning to teach in Nashville area schools for the next 25 years.

Nancy did not like the weather or the drinking and bathing water in Slidell since the water table was near the surface of the ground. It was very brackish and smelled awful. The only good thing was the monthly water bill totaled only $6.00 regardless of how much you used. We did love the Cajun cooking, our neighbors, and the local Methodist church that we joined because we were not too enthused with the Presbyterians in the deep south. I played the deciple Bartholomew in the Easter pageant one year. Nancy took a position at the local newspaper as a proofreader and stayed with it until we moved north.

We also had good times at the Kiwanis functions. At their many parties they had fresh crabs, shrimp, and vegetables boiled together in a large iron kettle over an outdoor fire along with a keg or two of all the Dixie beer you wanted to drink. I enjoyed playing football and basketball with the Kiwanians and their sponsored K Club young men as well as participating in other civic projects.

When I moved from my "comfort zone" in Washington, I did not know what I was getting into. I quickly found out that political influence ruled the day and the audit independence that I had known was severely handicapped. I learned from others that Agriculture's OIG was established in the early 1960s because of the Billy Sol Estes scandal concerning government loans received for grain crops that did not exist. Each Agricultural Agency in the 60s had their own audit groups and some lacked needed independence. Thus OIG was formed with its chief official (the Inspector General) reporting to the Secretary of Agriculture.

At the time I transferred, in 1973, OIG was eliminated and the Office of Audit (OA) and the Office of Investigations (OI) Directorates were established and reported to the Assistant Secretary of Agriculture for Administrations. The National Finance Office (NFC) also reported to this Assistant Secretary. Fundamentally this one person, the Assistant Secretary, had control over all financial transactions as well as auditing and conducting investigations pertaining to them. Audit lost much of its independence.

The following officials dictated accounting and auditing procedures and operations, resulting in a great impact on the effectiveness of our audits and relationships among all parties:

Assistant Secretary for Administration: Joe Wright. Remained in this position for one year while I was in New Orleans. He then left Government service and entered a business that had contracts with USDA.

Deputy Assistant Secretary for Administration: J. Paul Bolduc. Assumed Joe Wright's position when Wright departed. Boldock was a USDA auditor prior to working for Joe Wright. He had been a GS 14 in the New York Regional OIG office. Bolduc had a dictatorial manner and had no regard for me since I was told that he would not approve my promotion to GS 14 in New Orleans.

Director of Audit, Hq. USDA: Leonard Greess. Reported to the Assistant Secretary for Administration, He administered audit operations nationwide.

Director of the National Finance Center (NFC): Dennis Boyd. Reported to the Assistant Secretary for Administration. He was an effective administrator and a reasonable person who orchestrated the consolidation of all USDA payments and receipts into one central accounting department. After I left New Orleans, he returned to Washington under "cloudy" circumstances.

Southwest Regional Audit Director, Temple, Texas: Steve Jones. Reported to Leonard Greess. Steve Jones played politics to the maximum extent by being too chummy with the people we were auditing, by "watering down" important findings, by not going to bat for his auditors even though they were right, and by managing the Region as a "dictator". Phil Clark, a friend from Washington, who attended one of our conferences advised me to leave when I had the first chance. He was appalled at the way he saw Jones acting at the meeting.

Southwest Regional Assistant Audit Director, Temple, Texas: R. L. Cockrell. R. L. was a good person but played the political game of being the yes man for his immediate supervisor. R. L. became the Audit Director after Steve Jones retired

I wrote the following memo for record on June 10, 1975, that describes the politics and in fighting that went on between the above officials and the lack of control over accounting or audit operations.

"Power Play:
Dennis Boyd - Dir. NFC (GS - 17)
J. Paul Bolduc - Deputy. Asst. Secretary (Admin)

Dennis Boyd noted to me that J. P. Bolduc was trying to harass him through audit channels. Bolduc had tried, through Boyd's boss, the

Assistant Secretary, to no avail. Boyd noted the memos that were unsigned between him and Bolduc.

During this two to three month period, Hqs. requested two audits:--

> --Working Capital Funds (WCF)
> --Economic Analysis on Data Input.

Boyd did not want either audit. I made his wishes known to Steve Jones on the WCF and Joe Philibert wrote a memo to Jones on the Economic Analysis Evaluation—

> --Jones after talking with Len Greess delayed the WCF audit

> ---Joe Philibert recommended that the Economic
> Analysis be dropped.--It was.

It appears apparent that OAs position had been compromised. The ability to audit certain records will not be performed if the auditee resists the audit. On the other hand, the Deputy Asst. Secretary may continue to levy audit requirements that NFC will resist. The result is-- the Sub office will suffer.

Alternatives--

--Replace the sub office supervisor. I feel that this will not resolve the problem. (It didn't)

--Place sub office under OA Hqs.--This action should improve audit credibility as Region will not confront NFC management when a crisis arrives."

Nothing was done.

I had a good staff, John Weaver and Anita Smith had been auditors for several years and were proficient in their jobs. John retired after I left and went to work for Steve Jones in the Soloman Islands for a year or two.

Anita left audit and went to work at the Center. In the three years that I was there we had auditors coming and going all the time. One was Bob Sanders who was riffed from the Air Force the same year I was. He stayed with Agriculture for a couple more years then left to take a job with TVA in Tennessee. I was very fortunate to have two young auditors on the staff who had just arrived before me. Brad Womack was a native of New Orleans and Joe Cantu was from Texas. They were very proficient in using software packages such as STRATA, Easy Trieve, etc. in monitoring newly established NFC payment and receipt systems being established; such as gasoline credit card, telephone, service and supply expenditures, etc.

Joe passed all parts of the CPA examination the first time he took it.--quite an accomplishment!

Just before I left for Kentucky, I called John Davis who worked for me at Barksdale and recommended Joe for a job with Texas Gas Pipeline where John was now an official. Joe was interviewed and moved back to Houston and was happy to be away from the NFC.

Brad left audit and took a job with NFC and became head of the accounting section that issued salary checks nation-wide twice a month. NFC later took over other agency payrolls and paid millions of Government employees their salaries.. He remained with NFC until he retired.

Besides monitoring the creation of the above mentioned NFC systems, we furnished auditors in many states with listings like I used on my prior job in Food Stamp audits. We worked with USDA Investigators when we converted hand written certificates that inspectors prepared when they inspected grain ship and barge cargos to punch cards for computer input and found fraudulent inspections. As a result, USDA formed a Federal Inspection Group to assure that all required inspections were made.

One of the most interesting things that Brad worked on was a delayed employee pay raise in the payroll system. There was a computer glitch that caused over 4,000 workers to be overpaid. Several thousand dollars were recovered. Dennis Boyd was really impressed with this finding.

When Steve Jones came to the Center from Temple he would meet with Dennis Boyd and often I would not know what was discussed. About a year after I arrived, Joe Wright and Steve Jones met with Dennis Boyd (I was not invited) and when Wright questioned Boyd's actions and shortcomings, Boyd told Wright that Bill Lively's crew was performing lots of audit work that did not involve the Center so he was not getting the audit support he needed. The next week Joe Cantu and I were in Temple with Steve Jones preparing an audit program to be followed that would cover the Center thoroughly. A few months later, in front of Andy Best from our Washington headquarters, Boyd asked me to leave him alone and go audit someone else.

On July 31, 1975, Steve Jones and Bill Forsythe, out of Washington, had lunch with me and stated the following that I recorded in my log:

"I stand no chance for the GS 14 (promotion). Forsythe felt that my promotion would not be approved at the Asst. Sec. level. OA officials were satisfied with my performance. Forsythe stated that if I stayed in N. O. the new man may be here for a short time and I could be considered again. He also asked me about moving to St. Louis. I informed them I would like to go to Ky. Forsythe and Jones visited Boyd later and Boyd stated we are doing a good job and it was inferred that Boyd said that he was happy that Lively was getting promoted" HA HA.

Since my time in New Orleans was limited, around the first of October I talked with John Yazurlo at HUD and he said that I would be in the top four for a similar GS 14 job in Washington. I also talked with General Bob Presley and sent him an application Form 171. During the second week of October we had a regional conference and Bolduc "built up" the NO Sub Office (per my log). Later I talked with Len Greess and told him I would probably leave and go with HUD or the Air Force. On October 15, I talked with Yazurlo and turned down his HUD Job. Later I talked with Bob Presley. -He would get me a GS 14 in Air Force Budget Division in the Pentagon.

On January 14, 1976, The Comptroller General was in New Orleans for a conference and most Federal Agencies had their top staff there. At a cocktail party later that evening, John Yazurlo offered me a job in the Columbus HUD audit office since I turned down his GS 14 job in Washington. Len Greess noticed that I was talking with John Yazurlo and promptly asked me if I was interested in Kentucky. My answer was affirmative. Two days later Mr. Greess visited my office and said he would get my transfer to Kentucky started and I would hear from him soon. On January 22, Mr. Yazurlo called and stated he was announcing the Columbus job. He suggested I apply for it, and take it if Leonard Greess did not come through.

After many delays and questions of whether I would go to Columbus with HUD or to the Kentucky sub office; on April 19, Phil Clark my buddy who told me earlier to leave Steve Jones region called and said I had been picked for Kentucky. The next day Jones called and stated that I had been selected to be in the Southeast Region on May 10. HOOOOray!

After transferring to Kentucky, on September 28, 1977, The Comptroller General issued a report to congress, entitled "Computer Auditing in the Executive Departments; Not Enough is Being Done." It was very critical of most agencies but complimented our audit performed by Joe Cantu in auditing the test phase of a proposed subsystem three months before planned implementation.

When I sent this report to Joe, he wrote of his feelings concerning our tenure at the New Orleans Sub Office. Excerpts from his letter follow:

"I don't think you and I ever convinced Steve Jones we were trying to do an important job in a difficult area and situation..---Speaking of Steve Jones, the EDP Auditor's Association, Houston Chapter, where I am a member, had the International conference here in July. The Dept of Agriculture had about five people attend, one of whom was Steve Jones, would you believe. John Weaver and the new GS 14 from New Orleans who used to be with HUD were also there. I have to say, Bill, the new GS 14 didn't impress me, running around pampering Jones. Jones, of course, ate it up. The fellow from N.O. even tried to get smart with me making comments about Dennis Boyd and our former audit work. I talked to Jones while we were at one of the more boring workshop sessions. He told me how much more improved the N.O. office was, how much work was getting produced, and how much more disciplined the office environment had become.

Jones must have forgotten that I was part of the old crew he was telling me about because I didn't like it and I told him so. I said, I never had any problems with you because I liked you, respected you, and did what I was told. I then went on to tell him that the disciplined approach he was talking about is OK for a couple of people in the office who didn't give a damn, but for my attitude your management style was beautiful. Namely, that being, you would tell me what you wanted done, I'd figure out how to do it and try to do it correctly. I told him that was the management approach professional audit managers give professional caliber employees He didn't touch on that subject again after that."

Over the years, I found that several of my colleagues knew of my problems in New Orleans and felt that the job got done as well as could be done under the circumstances. Over the next nine years of my USDA service I never heard of any significant audit that came out of that sub office. So I guess the auditors there just went with the flow. A few years later I was part of a study team to determine if there should be a special Division for NFC and Computer audit staffs headed by a GS 15. To many of the folks surprise, I thought it would be a bad idea.

CHAPTER 10

Kentucky May 1976 - March 1985

Twas the tenth day of May in '76,
I came home to live in my Kentucky "sticks,"

Once we were back I was here to stay,
And never regretted it for one single day.

I arrived in Mercer County (Harrodsburg) on the tenth, moved in with
cousin Mary Anne Sharpe and her girls for a month or so, and commuted
daily to the sub-office in Lexington. Nancy, Leonard, and Billy arrived in
June after the Slidell school year ended and we settled in Earnest Hager's
house on Herrington Lake until we bought our home in Burgin which
was across the street from my cousin Bush Peavler. Mike joined us soon
after we moved in. In September, Len and Billy started school up the street
from our house and fit right in with their classmates. Len was a senior and
Billy was in the eight grade. Jan had just graduated from college and began
her teaching career in the mountain town of Hazard, Kentucky. The next
year she moved back to the Nashville area and has been there ever since.

We joined the Presbyterian Church in Danville and remained there for
about five years until we moved our membership to Harrodsburg United
Presbyterian where we still cherish, serve and belong. Nancy and I became
Elders, choir members, kitchen workers, auditor, and any other duty called
for. Through these years the friends we made in this old church has been
wonderful.

Nancy began working at the Danville Advocate newspaper and later worked at the old Harrodsburg Fort Harrod (State Park) sewing quilts in a cabin and later as a museum guide until 1992.

Len graduated from High School in 1977 and entered college at Western Kentucky State University in Bowling Green that year. After one year his old boss in Slidell asked him to come back to Louisiana and manage another theatre he was building. So, Len has been in the theatre business ever since.

Billy finished high school in 1981 where he had taken industrial arts classes, then entered Morehead State University for a couple of years until he started installing kitchen cabinets and other wood cabinets, etc. as a master craftsman ever since.

Mike has stayed in the area and now resides in Junction City with Barbra his wife for over fifteen years. They have been a wonderful help to Nancy and me and his grandmother Jessie who resided in a nursing home in Harrodsburg before she passed away in 2011.

After returning to Kentucky, we picked up relationships with our old Louisville buddies: Don and Kaye Pugh; coaches Wood, Camp, Gitscher, and Trabue; teammates John Unitas, Jim Williams, Jim Wolf, Jack Gilliam, Walter Crawford, Jim Fults, Bob Lichvar, and many others at football games, Homecomings, and other gatherings. We had a wonderful relationship with Nancy's Chi O sister Barbara and her husband Clifton Rhodes who resided in Danville and became close with my cousin Pierce Lively and his wife, Amelia.

It was great to be back home with my Peavler cousins--Bush, Eva, Morris, H. L., Mary Anne and their families. It was also only a two or three hour drive to Louisville, Cincinnati, or Nashville to be with Nancy's family.

The nine years I spent in the Lexington sub office were really enjoyable most of the time. I again had two great young auditors assigned to my seven auditor staff that confirmed an anonymous quotation stating, "Success happens by surrounding yourself with young people who do not know that it cannot be done." This is so true. Mic Duncan and Tom Dantic were inergetic, intelligent, creative and could communicate proficiently. Tom remained in the office for a couple of years and then was promoted, and transferred to Washington. Mic stayed in Lexington during my entire nine years, then was transferred to supervise the sub office in Raleigh, North Carolina.

Soon after my arrival, good friends Charlie Reiser and Jimmy McDonald transferred to Atlanta as Regional Inspector General (RIG) and assistant (ARIG). I could not ask for any better bosses since I had worked closely with them during my tenure in the Washington area. Charlie remained the RIG for about four years until the Reagan Administration forced him to retire in 1980. Jimmy was still assigned as my boss until I retired in 1985.

In 1978, Atlanta had an ARIG (GS 14) vacancy and Charlie asked if I would like to come to Atlanta for a promotion. He had just awarded me a Certificate of Merit, with a cash award, so I could probably have had the job. It took me about two minutes to say no thank you, since I had returned to Kentucky and had no reason to leave. I'm certainly glad that I turned it down because Charlie's successor as RIG in 1980, Steady Mixon was not a kind of person I would want to work with closely. I still don't know how Jimmy got along with him. He was a poor manager.

During the nine years in the Lexington Sub office, We performed audits in all the Agriculture programs. We did many audits of Food Stamp, Farmers Home, School Lunch, ASCS and other programs. One audit of the Louisville Food Stamp Program disclosed that known offenders of the program discovered in prior audits were still drawing food stamps monthly. In the northern counties of Kentucky we found that recipients were drawing food stamps there and also were participating in the Cincinnati FS Program across the river. At the State level we questioned the practice of having thousands of authorization (ATP) cards punched and re-keypunched before and after they were cashed for stamps. We also matched FSP records with the State police records showing alias names. An official at Atlanta's Food and Nutrition Service complimented our office as having cleaned the State's program while I was here.

Before Charlie Reiser retired we initiated a National audit of Farmer Home's Community Program loans and grants to community's water and sewer systems, hospitals, fire stations, and other similar projects. Just after we started Steady Mixon replaced Charlie as RIG and our problems began. It took us about two months to do the field work, but about six months to get the report out because of all the writes and rewrites caused mainly by Mixon.

We had very significant findings that included the following:

$8.1 loans and grants to two borrowers in densely populated areas rather than low to moderate income rural populations;

Overbuilding, planning or operational problems in eleven projects causing excessive costs of$3.8 million;

One 25 mile pipeline installed in a desolate, undeveloped desert area;

Contractors failed to install safe, serviceable equipment, account for materials billed to projects (referred to investigation), and conform to plans and specifications;

Resident inspectors did not report problems on seven projects $683,000 loss;

Engineering firms' fees in 24 projects were excessive --exceeded normal rates by $3.4 million;

44 obligations totaling $11.0 million should be cancelled since the project had had been cancelled or funded from other sources

Usually an exit conference with Agency officials lasts about one to two hours. This conference lasted 5 days in Washington. Farmers Home was represented by 9 Headquarters staff and 6 State community program chiefs. Audit was represented by one GS 13 Headquarters officer, as an observer, myself and 7 auditors. During the weeklong session the Agency

Administrator Dwight Calhoun, huddled with his representatives in the hall to determine their strategy in responding to our findings.

After the weeklong session we received FmHA answers. to our findings and recommendations. We attached our rebuttals where needed and three months later the report was finally issued.

Two years later Dwight Calhoun received a $20,000 Distinguished Senior Executive award from President Reagan. The award cited that, "he has promoted major economies in the management of rural water and waste facilities through loan programs, and under his direction program regulations have been revised to ensure the availability of loans to poor communities."

I guess we got our point across!

On April 18, 1985; I was 55 years old, had 30 years and 15 days Federal Service, and was thoroughly disgusted with the direction OIG Audit was headed. So, I officially retired and never regretted my decision. Since then the sub office along with other sub offices were closed. Very few, if any, auditors have set foot in the State in the last 25 years.

The End

EPILOGUE

It has been many years since I started this Bio. and now Nancy and I are back in Louisville at a great retirement community called Brownsboro Park. We decided on moving in September 2013, told Brownsboro Management in October that we would move by November 14. We returned home to Burgin and immediately placed our home on the market. The first persons who came to our home bought it. So, in five weeks, with the help of all our children we settled in our apartment on November 14, 2013. It is great to be back in Louisville.

Lets go back to 1985 when I retired from Agriculture. After retirement I piddled at several jobs to keep from being bored. Lets see, I worked for a couple of years at Freeman & Ison's Men Store where I could get nice clothes at bargain prices, then spent a couple of months working at the old Shakertown Community but had questions on how it was run so resigned. Later, I participated in the 1990 census in Mercer and Woodford Counties, loved being out in the field. After the census I worked for the Property Valuation Commission in Mercer County for about a year traveling all over the county measuring houses and out buildings for County tax purposes.

In 1991, Jimmy Mc Donald called and said he was working for a Government contractor doing cost audits in New Orleans, and would I be interested. I said yes, so for the next two years I performed audits at the US Department Of Energy's Strategic Petroleum Reserves in New Orleans and Fernald Atomic Plant in Cincinnati, Ohio. About that time Nancy developed breast cancer, so my working days all over the country came to an end and I was ready for it.

The years since 1985 have been anything but boring--

--For several years we spent about a week each late spring with Cousin Morris Peavler, his brother and sister and their spouses on a house boat on lake Cumberland, great times;

--Over the years we always made trips to Florida each January or February to see Len, cousins Pierce Lively, Alice Benner and Jimmy Dorsey;

---I was in several plays acting and singing in the local community theatre; and

--Nancy and I were actively involved with our United Presbyterian Church in Harrodsburg both serving as Elders, choir members, activity chairmen, and auditing church financial records.

We developed lasting friendships with wonderful people in the thirty something years of our retirement--

--I was on the search committee to find a new pastor and the committee selected Joe Tarry who served until his untimely death in 2006. We were very close. Joe, his wife Elaine, Nancy and I had many sojourns together. Joe and I even drove to Louisville together to see the Cardinals beat Florida State in a torrential rain. Joe and I had another buddy named Clyde Jackson, a retired school principal, a great story teller and piano player, who also passed away soon after Joe.

-- Church members: Sue Sullivan: Margaret and her Baptist husband and retired Kentucky State Police Officer Jim Fitzgerald; Jackie Lindberg; Henry and Conchita Grall ; Elaine and Ralph Lipps; and Mary and David Weber had lunch after church each Sunday. Our group also had many outings such as: attending races at Churchill Downs and the Red Mile in Lexington; concerts in the park; wine tasting; home parties for ball games, Christmas, 4th of July, the Run for the Roses; and birthdays.

--Nancy and I really got to know cousin Pierce over the last few years, after his lovely wife Amelia passed away. We always enjoyed our time with him in Florida and at home in Danville. He and I were of the same mind when we discussed what was happening in the world through good times and bad. Nancy even calls Pierce her favorite cousin.

We are very proud of our immediate family. And through good times and bad we were so fortunate that no one had serious illnesses or life threatening accidents occurr in the sixty years of our being together.

Jan, our oldest, her husband Alex Zanetis, her three sons Jordan, Adam and Will have prospered over the years--

--Alex as an accomplished musician, song and screen writer;

--Jan an educator and presently the CEO of a company that provides distance learning through the computer and internet services to students worldwide;

--Jordan, her oldest son, has completed college and seminary education to be a Greek Orthodox Priest;

-- Adam, her second, obtained a law degree in Florida and now practices in Madison, Tennessee.

--Will, the youngest, graduated from Western Kentucky University and currently travels all over the country selling ads for a company who publishes magazines that promote and highlight cities.

Mike and Barbra reside in Junction City, Kentucky and spend most of their time helping others in need as well as being care givers to Nancy and me in our old age.

Bill is a master woodworker and cabinet maker and installer and his wife Pauline who is on Eastern Kentucky University staff are active in their church activities. Their son Thomas has graduated from Eastern and is currently seeking employment.

Leonard and his wife Amanda reside in Destin, Florida. He is still in the movie theater business and will be until he retires. They have three daughters and one grandson, our only great grandson named Samuel. They are--

--Brittany, Sal and Samuel Montalto. Sal and his family have a great restaurant in Fort Walton Beach and Brittany will be hair stylist;

--Rebecca is currently in college working toward a Communication Degree;

-- Danielle is a high school senior.

In my 84 years I have been fortunate to always seem to be at the right place at the right time. When things go bad you walk through the wilderness but the light at the end has always turned up and more than often the bad things turn out well. If I wore a crown the friendships made would be shining stars that would adorn it. Those beautiful people mentioned above would be the stars and the following stars would make my crown so heavy that at my age would be too heavy. I'm sure that I will miss many folks that are my stars, but to the best I can I will list the ones that are truly dear to me.

1930s

My Mother and Father --Eva Peavler Lively and Thomas Lively
My Brother-- Thomas Lively
Aunt Vera and Uncle Henry Bush
Uncle Morris and Aunt Lill Peavler
Uncle Byron and Aunt Laura and their children Bush, Eva, Morris, H.L., and Mary Anne
Granddad Leonard Peavler
Jim, John, George, Bill and Frank Ellers
Uncle Gene and Aunt Lizzie Lively
Dr. Gaines Dobbins

1940s, 50s & 60s

Grade & High School Buddies--
   Sammy Edwards, T.C. Coleman, Bacon Moore, Billy Willey, David Roach, Frank Yeast, Lawrence Willis, Kathryn Sanders, Doris Merriman, Sitty Russell, Betty Dennis, Mary Anne Peavler

Employers and co workers--
   Archie Woods, Larry Rice, Harold Sutherland

Legends I lived with, played for, or played with--
   Jack Coleman, Coach Aggie Sales, Coach Clark Wood, John Unitas

Louisville teammates, especially--
   Jack Gillam, Jim Fults, Walter Crawford, Dave Rivenbark, Don Pugh, Jim Willliams, Amos Black, Bob Lichvar

College Friends--
   Dean John Craf, Coaches Frank Camp, J D Dunn, and Joe Trabue, NANCY and her sorority sisters, Warren Oates, Dave Jones, Bernie Myers, T Lee Adams, Charlene & Bill Penny, Tom & Marilyn Ramey

Air Force Friends--
   The Burk Beros, Ed Kimbals, Jack Rashes, Ken Beckners, Ken Hills, Floyd Jacks, Jim Jordans, my accounting office staffs in Munich and Weisbaden, Jack Annelli, Bob Storrs, Pete Morretta,

Relatives and Neighbors--
   F. C. Dorsey, Hiram & Jessie Dorsey, Linda & Billy Gaw, Jim, Evelyn, Alice & Jimmie Dorsey, Barbara & Stirling Moore, Libba Tharp

1970s, 80s & 90s

Air Force Friends--
   Frank & Jo Anne Nusspickle, Jerry Solecki, Pat & Kathy Jones,
   Jim Baker, Peg & Stark Sanders, John & Brenda Davis, Joe White,
   Bobby Pressley, Millie Engle

Dept of Agricultural Friends--
   Bill Dickson, Jimmie Mc Donald, Charles Bremer, Brad Womack,
   Joe Cantu, Joe Fisch, Hubie Sparks, Mic Duncan, Hank Eblin,
   Charles Reiser, Dennis Zimmerman

All the above folks have remained friends through the years and I would
consider them Stars for my crown, if I had one. The greatest friend I have
is the love of my life NANCY! The last thing on my mind or lips when I
pass will be Nanny.

FINISHED

Bill Lively
March 7, 2014

Printed in the United States
By Bookmasters